W9-AEM-385

Puzzles and Pieces in Wonderland

The Promise and Practice of Student Affairs Research

Karl J. Beeler
Deborah Ellen Hunter
editors

National Association of Student Personnel Administrators, Inc.
1875 Connecticut Avenue, NW
Suite 418
Washington, D.C. 20009-5728
202/265-7500

Library of Congress Cataloging-in-Publication Data
Puzzles and pieces in wonderland: the promise and practice of student affairs research / Karl J. Beeler, Deborah Ellen Hunter, editors.
        p. cm.
    Includes bibliographical references.
    ISBN: 0-931654-16-5 : $7.95
    1. Personnel service in higher education — Research — United States. 2. Education, Higher — Research — United States. I. Beeler, Karl J. II. Hunter, Deborah Ellen
LB2343.P89 1991   91-27478
378'.0072—dc20   CIP

Other Titles in the NASPA Monograph Series

The Role of Student Affairs in Institution-Wide Enrollment Management Strategies

The Invisible Leaders: Student Affairs Mid-Managers

The New Professional: A Resource Guide for New Student Affairs Professionals and Their Supervisors

From Survival to Success: Promoting Minority Student Retention

Student Affairs and Campus Dissent: Reflection of the Past and Challenge for the Future

Alcohol Policies and Procedures on College and University Campuses

Opportunities for Student Development in Two-Year Colleges

Private Dreams, Shared Visions: Student Affairs Work in Small Colleges

Translating Theory into Practice: Implications of Japanese Management Theory for Student Personnel Administrators

Risk Management and the Student Affairs Professional

Career Perspectives in Student Affairs

Contents

Contributors *vii*

Preface *viii*

Chapter 1
The Promise of Student Affairs Research
Karl J. Beeler and Deborah Ellen Hunter 1
Each campus is a unique Wonderland, complex and exciting. Campus-based student affairs research is a key to greater understanding of students, campus environments, and planning and policy issues.

Chapter 2
In Search of the Lost Chord: Applying Research to Planning and Decision Making
Larry G. Benedict 18
By simplifying the language of research and keeping the needs of the decision maker in mind, research can usually be made useful, timely, and cost effective. Examples of efficient and useful data-gathering techniques used by selected student affairs practitioners are cited.

Chapter 3
Of Puzzles and Pieces: Organizing and Directing a Campus-Based Research Agenda
William H. Weitzer and Gary D. Malaney 35
Answering a few guiding questions before launching into research saves time and money. Selected research strategies are described and grouped by required levels of expertise and cost.

Chapter 4
Rethinking Research in Student Affairs
George D. Kuh 55
Different approaches to research in higher education are needed. Conventional modes of inquiry are contrasted with alternatives. Research contributions using naturalistic inquiry or combining quantitative and qualitative methods are discussed.

Chapter 5
The Call to Assessment: What Role for Student Affairs?
Gary Hanson 80

The assessment movement has created new opportunities for student affairs professionals to assume pivotal campus roles. Three major purposes of assessment are explored and inherent methodological issues are addressed. New strategies are offered for assessing student development outcomes.

Chapter 6
Peering Through the "Looking Glass" at Preparation Needed for Student Affairs Research
Deborah Ellen Hunter and Karl J. Beeler 106

A socialization framework is needed to make research appealing and useful to graduate students and seasoned professionals alike. Suggestions for restructuring curricular offerings in student affairs preparation programs and developing research competencies among practitioners are highlighted.

Chapter 7
Student Affairs Research on Trial
Robert D. Brown 124

Research is an obligation, not a frill. A tireless proponent and national leader in student affairs research examines the profession's past performance, passes judgment, and offers specific advice for improving in the exciting years ahead.

Contributers

Karl J. Beeler, Assistant to the Vice Chancellor for Student Affairs, University of Missouri - St. Louis, St. Louis, Missouri

Larry G. Benedict, Vice President for Student Affairs, University of Southern Maine, Portland, Maine

Robert D. Brown, Professor of Education, University of Nebraska, Lincoln, Nebraska

Gary Hanson, Research Coordinator, University of Texas at Austin, Austin, Texas

Deborah Ellen Hunter, Assistant Professor of Higher Education and Student Affairs, University of Vermont, Burlington, Vermont

George D. Kuh, Professor of Higher Education, Indiana University, Bloomington, Indiana

Gary D. Malaney, Director of Student Affairs Research and Evaluation Office, University of Massachusetts, Amherst, Massachusetts

William H. Weitzer, Vice Provost, Wesleyan University, Middletown, Connecticut

Preface

Paradoxically, research in student affairs organizations is at once a highly promoted yet vastly underutilized activity. Somewhere between its theoretical promise and its actual practice, student affairs research falls prey to anxiety, busy schedules, and reactionary management. Although research skills are unquestionably among those needed to make effective and practical planning, policy, and management decisions, studies of student affairs research and evaluation activities in American colleges and universities have clearly demonstrated that research is practiced only to a moderate extent by professional members.

Many reasons have been offered for the profession's failure to live up to its own standards of research practice and those of others within academe. The feeble excuses and outright misconceptions that research is too time consuming, costly, or abstract are challenged throughout this monograph. The more palpable explanations—that research is misunderstood, poorly planned, and rarely applied to decision making—are systematically addressed within this publication. The contributing authors are well versed in the potential benefits of student affairs research, but more important, they are each well practiced in the application of research to student affairs administration.

The choice of *Alice's Adventures in Wonderland* as an allegorical reference in discussing student affairs research serves two purposes. One, of course, is to enliven the topic of research for those who still view it as anxiety-ridden or uninteresting. The second purpose is to draw some fundamental parallels between the Wonderland environment as Alice experienced it, and the campus environment as the student affairs professional might perceive it. In drawing from Alice's adventures, the editors and authors hope to illustrate how many delightful similarities exist between Wonderland and the campus environment, and how the search for meaning and direction in higher education and student affairs seems so poignantly comparable to the wanderings of Alice.

Readers may also think of students and of student affairs professionals as having much in common with Alice, whose growth is naturally accompanied by turmoil and upset. Rather than a fanciful escape into unbridled imagination, this use of Lewis Carroll's popular tale is meant to encourage readers to envision campus environments as mysterious and complex places to explore, with fascinating characters to study.

This monograph was written to address the concerns of practitioners (youthful and experienced), students, and graduate preparation faculty who want to know how research can be made interesting, affordable, relevant, and useful in student affairs. It is intended to provide a memorable overview of research issues; a practical guide to conducting and teaching about research; and a challenging critique of current research assumptions, methods, and practices.

In Chapter One, Beeler and Hunter clarify the similarities between Wonderland and the campus environment, introduce ways in which research can be viewed as a practical tool, and argue for more and better research based on the characteristics of students at the individual campus level. Examples of research questions that ought to be of concern to all postsecondary institutions are cited, along with a theoretical discussion of the use of research and an actual case study of how research is used to inform planning and decision making in student affairs at one university.

In Chapter Two, Benedict lists reasons commonly cited for failing to conduct research in student affairs, argues for simplifying the language of research, and shows that research need not be expensive or time consuming. He reminds the reader that every practitioner is a decision maker and gives actual examples of how professionals in health education, orientation, residential life, career counseling, financial aid, admissions, and enrollment management have gathered and used data at low cost to make better decisions.

In Chapter Three, Weitzer and Malaney describe a simple four-step process for planning the design of research projects and discuss the important issues of cost and level of expertise needed to complete selected types of research. Their discussion includes descriptions of innovative research strategies taking into account needed levels of expertise. They explain such strategies as interpreting existing reports, informal discussion and observation, interpreting comparative studies, using external surveys with external analysis, computer analysis of existing data, trend analysis, content analysis, focus groups, external surveys with in-house analysis, database analysis, telephone surveys, mail surveys, formal observation, and face-to-face interviews. As it is organized, this chapter also serves as a practical guide for assessing needed expenditures and personnel before committing research resources to a given project.

In Chapter Four, Kuh presses the profession to move forward in its thinking about what constitutes useful knowledge and how related information can be gathered. He begins by summarizing the need for different approaches to research in higher education, then describes and compares conventional modes of inquiry with alternative approaches. Kuh cites some contributions to be made by naturalistic inquiry to studying and understanding issues of student life and developmental processes. He also discusses the possibility of combining quantitative and qualitative methods of research, using as examples two well-known studies from the student development literature.

In Chapter Five, Hanson provides a thorough and demystified overview of assessment issues in higher education and student affairs. He begins by explaining why higher education has become a focal issue and how assessment can be used to serve both accountability and the need to improve daily practice. He explores three major purposes of assessment—diagnosis, monitoring, and evaluation—and delves into the methodological issues inherent in the assessment of student development outcomes.

Hanson stresses the importance of using appropriate assessment methods, and challenges the profession to develop more relevant assesssment instruments. He offers several new strategies for assessing student development outcomes. Finally, he explains how the assessment movement has created a new opportunity for student affairs professionals to assume pivotal campus roles, capitalizing on the profession's experience and knowledge base.

In Chapter Six, Hunter and Beeler discuss how student affairs professionals can be motivated and taught the skills needed for competency in research methods and applications. A socialization framework is used to explain current problems in learning about or using research and to suggest ways to make research appealing to graduate students and practitioners alike. Increased opportunities for involvement and early success are stressed, along with systematic efforts to underscore the importance of research in curricular offerings for graduate students and continuing education for student affairs professionals. Questions are posed as guides for graduate faculty who wish to restructure curricula to develop research competencies and for professional associations which strive to rekindle members' orientations toward research.

In Chapter Seven, Brown draws on years of experience as distinguished professor of educational psychology, researcher, author, editor of a major student affairs journal, and president of a student affairs professional association to pass judgment on the profession as a producer and user of research.

A tireless proponent of the increased use and overall improvement of student affairs research, Brown points unabashedly to where the profession has been found wanting and offers specific advice for doing better in the years ahead. He has characterized the use of research in student affairs as an obligation, not a frill. Perhaps the preeminent spokesman for this sentiment, his words echo loud and clear through the halls and gardens of campus Wonderlands everywhere.

Chapter 1

The Promise of Student Affairs Research

Karl J. Beeler
Deborah Ellen Hunter

"Would you tell me, please, which way I ought to go from here?" said Alice.

"That depends a good deal on where you want to get to," said the Cat.

"I don't much care where . . .," said Alice.

"Then it doesn't matter where you go," said the Cat.

" . . . so long as I get somewhere," Alice added as an explanation.

"Oh, you're sure to do that," said the Cat, "if only you walk long enough."

Alice's Adventures in Wonderland
Chapter VI: Pig and Pepper

Alice's adventures in Wonderland are remarkably like a day in the life of a student affairs practitioner on any college campus. Alice's search for identity and direction among the curious inhabitants of Wonderland has a ring of familiarity to student affairs professionals who labor to understand their place and to find appropriate direction within one of society's most complex institutions.

From a management perspective, few would argue that moving a student affairs organization in a productive direction requires knowing "where you want to get to." However, in colleges and universities, as in Wonderland, it is a challenge to establish the right direction and easy to lose one's way. As the Cheshire cat suggests, there are but two choices in this quandary: keep walking or search out a destination.

Wonderland Revisited

Lewis Carroll's classic tale, *Alice's Adventures in Wonderland,* is the story of a young girl who, on an afternoon outing with her sister in the bucolic English countryside, falls into deep slumber on a warm river bank and dreams of a fantastic sojourn through the curious subterranean world, Wonderland.

As the tale begins, Alice is growing sleepy watching her older sister read a book with "no pictures or conversations in it." In that imaginative, drowsy moment just before sleep, Alice envisions a well-appointed white rabbit scurrying by, pulling a watch from its waistcoat pocket and proclaiming aloud, "Oh dear! Oh, dear! I shall be too late!"

Now fast asleep, Alice dreams she is chasing the time-obsessed hare, following it down a deep rabbit hole beneath a hedge. Inside, she tumbles down a seemingly endless tunnel to a dark passage, which she runs along until she finds herself in a long, well-lit hall lined with several locked doors. Finding a golden key on a nearby table, she tests each of the locks until, at last, she opens a door so small that she cannot pass through it. On the other side she can see a lovely garden, full of bright flowers and fountains, which she longs to enter.

The remainder of the tale chronicles Alice's adventures as she searches for a way into the garden. Along the way she meets and questions a succession of strange and surreal characters, including a large blue caterpillar smoking a hookah, a cruel duchess, a Cheshire cat, a March hare, and a mad hatter. Alice soon realizes these beings are quite unclear about their places in Wonderland and, therefore, are not particularly helpful in giving her directions. Preoccupied with immediate or past experiences, they pose meaningless riddles and relate bizarre oral histories. Her interactions with them only leave Alice more confused. By the time she meets the Cheshire cat, she is happy to have any directions at all.

Alice finally manages to enter the garden through the small doorway by eating bits of mushroom until she shrinks to the right size. Inside the garden, she is disappointed to realize that it bears little resemblance to the alluring environment she thought she had seen through the doorway. The bright flowers are only painted facades, and the garden is ruled by the cruel Queen of Hearts.

The predominant activity of the garden's inhabitants is an odd version of croquet in which the balls are little curled up hedgehogs, the mallets are live flamingoes held upside down, and the wickets are ordinary playing cards bent in arc-shaped postures. Playing the game is difficult because the wickets leave their assigned posts and stroll about the garden, only to assume a different position elsewhere.

Alice is understandably puzzled by the disorder of the garden. Having spent so much energy getting there, she is distraught to find no common sense of purpose or direction among the inhabitants. In language uncomfortably familiar to those who have witnessed the puzzling management of colleges and universities, Alice proclaims to the Cheshire cat, ". . . they all quarrel so dreadfully one can't hear oneself speak—and they don't seem to have any rules in particular: at least, if there are, nobody attends to them—and you've no idea how confusing it is . . . "

Alice's adventures culminate in a courtroom trial in which the Knave of Hearts is accused of stealing the queen's tarts. The courtroom is jammed with Wonderland's diverse characters, who act not only as witnesses but as members of the jury as well. Much pointless "evidence" is introduced, none of which forms the basis for an informed or reasoned verdict. Yet the queen continually presses the jury for a decision. As the tale ends, Alice, infuriated by the queen's attitude and the prevailing disregard for evidence, shatters the courtroom drone screaming, "Who cares for you? You're nothing but a pack of cards!"

Campus Wonderlands

High rates of attrition among student affairs administrators suggest that Alice's sentiment is widely shared in academe. It is easy to draw parallels between Wonderland and campus environments, between Alice and student affairs professionals. At most colleges and universities, student affairs practitioners receive little direction for managing enrollments, enhancing student life, or providing a comprehensive array of support services in an environment every bit as complex as Wonderland. Yet they are expected to make judicious decisions and demonstrate some measure of success. To do so, they must learn to appreciate complexity as a natural characteristic of postsecondary institutions and to anticipate confusion rather than react to it.

With this in mind, the similarities between postsecondary environments and Wonderland are not only entertaining but instructive:

- Diversity of mission and educational goals is alive and well (Carnegie, 1987, p. 2)
- There is great and ever-increasing diversity among students (Astin, Green & Korn, 1987, p. 10)
- Loose connections among individuals, processes, and units are the rule rather than the exception (Weick, cited in Kuh, 1983, p. 28)
- Decision making is a complex and rarely integrated process (Cooley & Bickel, 1986, p. 141)
- Forces for student development naturally produce turmoil and upset (Chickering, 1969, pp. 293-94)

Against this background of distinct missions, diverse players, loosely coupled organizations, complexity, and natural turmoil, it is hardly surprising that student affairs practitioners find it difficult to plan, implement, evaluate, or improve educational programs and services. Higher education administration often resembles a Wonderland croquet match: strategic shots by one player do not necessarily interest or engage other players. Indeed, there are no guarantees that activities are organized around a specific set of goals (Kuh, 1983, p. 17). Like Alice trying to play croquet, student affairs professionals are constantly challenged by ever-changing rules, equipment, and players.

There is also something about Alice's reactions that mirrors the collective experience of student affairs professionals. While she is obviously intelligent and practical, Alice nonetheless struggles to maintain her identity and direction among the other inhabitants of Wonderland. Perhaps it is her perpetual effort to make sense of the environment, to understand the characters who are in constant motion, or to stay abreast of the rules that change faster than she can learn them that bring the student affairs practitioner to mind. Alice's tendency to forge ahead in the face of uncertain circumstances, often without sufficient evidence to support her decisions, also strikes a familiar chord.

The Journey through Campus Wonderlands

To journey through Wonderland or college campuses, one must realize early that the environment is multidimensional. There has been notable discussion about the need for multiple perspectives in student affairs planning and decision making (Hull, Hunter & Kuh, 1983, p. 27). Yet the use of multiple sources of evidence to inform these perspectives has not been addressed.

Research as a Guidepost

Research and evaluation activities can help decision makers build informed perspectives and defensible decisions. Research counterbalances the tendency to rely too much on authority or conventional wisdom in making decisions (Beeler, Benedict & Weitzer, 1984, p. 8). In student affairs administration, as in Wonderland, overreliance on one perspective leads to shared ignorance and misdirection.

Planning and decision making in any applied profession invites serious reflection about those who are served and about the environment in which they live. Effective decisions must be responsive not only to the immediate needs of clients, but to the full ecology of their lives as well. For example, in treating patients for their personal illnesses, the responsible physician considers not only symptomatology and health history, but the potential influence of patients' living and working conditions. Similarly, in building solid cases for their clients, effective attorneys consider not only statutes, legal rights, and human behavior, but also the larger framework of legal precedents.

In this same vein, student affairs administrators, whose responsibilities include both student development and program management in a unique living and learning environment, must seek to understand a multiplicity of variables that influence the college student experience. Ideally, student affairs professionals plan, implement, and evaluate programs and services that not only address known characteristics and needs of enrolled students, but also consider the larger purposes of higher education, the distinct educational mission of the institution, and the environment in which students and educational mission converge.

Professionals in medicine, law, and education rely on several sources of information to make decisions:

- a body of theoretical or guiding principles
- common sense
- authority
- experience
- accumulated evidence.

The conscientious student affairs practitioner also draws from each of these sources, in effect using a wide system of checks and balances in formulating policies and decisions.

Within the student affairs profession, it is often alleged that research and evaluation are too esoteric or too difficult to apply to practical matters like balancing budgets or retaining staff members. Yet guiding a student affairs organization without research and evaluation evidence is like sailing the deepest seas only with elementary knowledge of navigation. Without proper regard for weather conditions, wave height, or destination, few student affairs professionals will long stay afloat. To ignore the need for reliable information about students and their experiences, about the campus environment, or about program effectiveness is to invite disaster.

Looking Twice at Student Affairs Research

Johnson and Steele (1984) studied student affairs research activity and attitudes at a random sample of 100 American colleges and universities, compiling some preliminary evidence that student affairs professionals do care about and conduct campus-based research and evaluation. Eighty-five percent of the schools responding to their survey reported that they are conducting research at least occasionally. However, most frequently this research is conducted by the counseling center, the department of residential life, the admissions or registrar office, the career guidance center, or the student activities program. Only about 10 percent of the student affairs divisions have an office whose main function is student affairs research, and these are found primarily in institutions with enrollments of 10,000 or more. These statistics suggest that research in student affairs divisions is typically a decentralized and disjointed process, conducted outside of division-wide coordination or concern for effective dissemination and utilization.

> Our findings demonstrate the extensiveness of student affairs research nationally, but they also indicate that at most schools the use of research results is quite modest. The impact of such results, for example, was primarily on individual programs . . . To enable student affairs research to have a university-wide impact, student affairs staff and administrators need to work at publicizing and promoting

the findings to university decision makers, who are often unaccustomed to using research results as input for decision making (Johnson & Steele, 1984, p. 204).

While it may be comforting to believe that student affairs research efforts are apparently widespread, there is no evidence to suggest that the body of this research is of high quality. Nor is there reason to believe that student affairs divisions take it upon themselves to evaluate the overall usefulness of their campus-based student affairs research. In light of these shortcomings, it is not surprising that this research has only limited impact at the organizational level at which it is produced. The true promise, or potential, of student affairs research can only begin to be realized when systematic efforts to encourage, review, assess, and apply research are forthcoming within the student affairs division.

A thoughtful and comprehensive research agenda cannot be formulated in the absence of division-wide support for organized student affairs research. If chief student affairs officers are willing to address the need for systematic inquiry, there will emerge an attendant expectation that professional staff use valid and reliable evidence to support their planning and programming decisions. If they do not, research will continue to be seen as secondary to decision making—as a luxury rather than guidance for decisions. This image is unacceptable in a profession that has so much riding on effectiveness. Brown (1986) argued that research in student affairs is essential.

> Research is not a frill. Research is a necessity and an obligation. Student affairs administrators have an obligation to their institutions, their students, and their profession to support research on their campuses. They should systematically collect data that help the institution engage in short- and long-range planning . . . (Brown, 1986, p. 195).

Research for Decision Making

Too often interest in research is stifled or extinguished because its purpose is misunderstood. Particularly in applied professions like student affairs, care must be taken to promote and design research that is relevant to the profession's purposes. If research is to be useful in managing student affairs organizations, it must be planned with decision makers' needs in mind. Prior to a discussion of decision-oriented research, it may be useful to review the distinctions between basic and applied research.

Basic research seeks knowledge for its own sake, without particular regard for its immediate application. This is the notion of research which most readily comes to mind when the word research is mentioned. It often elicits a reflexive negative reaction from educational administrators who claim to be "action oriented" (as opposed, presumably, to "research oriented").

Applied research, on the other hand, seeks to inform and influence immediate problems and short-term planning. In a discussion of the relevance of research to utilitarian ends, Tyler (1976) offered these distinctions between basic and applied research:

> With respect to the questions asked, basic research tends to differ from applied research in the fact that it is more concerned with "understanding" and the attainment of knowledge about fundamental variables and their relationships; the prediction of socially important phenomena is of secondary concern, arising solely out of the laws and relationships discovered . . . Applied research, however, is generally concerned with the control of socially significant phenomena or, if control is difficult or impossible, at least their prediction. It is interested in the "understanding" of phenomena in terms of laws and relationships as a basis for prediction and control (p. 9).

In recent years the concern that educational research and program evaluation be more focused on immediate applications to decision making has forced educators to reconsider models used to plan research. For example, Stufflebeam (1983) criticized the usefulness of program evaluation models available to guide mandatory evaluations of projects funded by the Elementary and Secondary Education Act of 1965 (ESEA). The prevalent model of educational evaluation at the time, the Tylerian model, focused only on assessing whether educational programs and services were meeting their stated goals and objectives. This strategy failed when applied to the assessment of ESEA projects because educators could not determine what student behaviors (outcomes) should result from these funded programs, and because the Tylerian approach ignored important program variables like context, available resources, and processes. Stufflebeam (1983) proposed as a reasonable alternative "that evaluation be redefined as a process of providing useful information for decision making" (p. 120).

Stufflebeam (1983) formulated a model of program evaluation to address the need for more systematic, formative types of program evaluation. His CIPP (context, input, process, product) model for program evaluation was one of the first attempts to assess programs for decision making (formative orientation), in addition to accountability (summative orientation). The CIPP model identifies four distinct objectives for program evaluation, depending on the needs of the stakeholders or decision makers (Stufflebeam, 1983, p. 121).

Today the ever-increasing demand to use research for immediate, utilitarian ends has given rise to added concern for the information needs of decision makers. Knowing just who uses research and what types of information they need is increasingly important in forming an organizational research agenda. Noting that Cronbach and Suppes divided the research world into conclusion-oriented and decision-oriented inquiry, Cooley and Bickel (1986) recently published an elaborate description of decision-oriented inquiry in educational systems in which they characterized such efforts as "research designed to help educators as they consider issues surrounding educational policy, as they establish priorities for improving educational systems, or as they engage in the day-to-day management of educational systems" (p. 3). They added,

> The distinguishing feature is that the research is guided by the information needs of the people responsible for that system. It is usually conducted by employees of an educational system or by researchers who are working closely with such systems and who have their research agendas established by the information needs of the educational system (p. 4).

Cooley and Bickel (1986) also stressed the importance of integrating decision-oriented educational research into policy and management processes. In their view, if research is to respond to the information needs of an educational system, the needs of the system must first be known and understood. A research capability that is truly integrated will influence action mechanisms for managing and improving operational performance (Cooley & Bickel, 1986, p. 10). Applied to student affairs organizations, this approach to educational research may go a long way toward addressing Brown's (1986) editorial injunction that "researchers in student affairs also have an obligation to see that the research they conduct is useful for administrative decision making . . . " (p. 195).

Pieces of the Puzzle

This monograph examines how applied, campus-based, decision-oriented research can provide information and directions for student affairs administrators in each college and university Wonderland. Each useful piece of student affairs research adds to a larger picture and a greater understanding of a particular college or university, contributing a new focus or a different perspective. Properly conceived, disseminated, and used, such research also helps to clarify the best directions for planning in a student affairs organization.

In student affairs administration, research questions which monitor student development or influence administrative decisions abound. The answers to these questions often raise more questions, thereby stimulating an informed dialogue within the institution. For example:

What are the characteristics and attributes of the student population at this institution? How do they compare with students in other American colleges and universities?

What are the general characteristics of this campus environment (physical and psychological) and what implications do they have for the development of these students?

What are the rates and correlates of retention at this institution?

What are the outcomes of a college education at this institution?

To what extent and in what manner are students at this institution involved in meaningful academic and cocurricular activities?

To what extent are programs and services of the student affairs division in compliance with professional standards? Are they achieving their stated goals and objectives? Are they effective? Efficient?

What are the educational and developmental needs of the student population? Of underrepresented or minority student populations?

How satisfied are students with their overall educational experience at this institution?

How can the quality of campus life be described?

What is the projected impact of changes in admissions standards? Recruiting processes? Marketing efforts? Pricing and financial aid?

What is the relationship of student clientele to stated mission, goals, and program?

The answers to these and other questions of concern to student affairs professionals are evidence and feedback for planning and recycling decisions. By monitoring trends in these areas, practitioners gain an informed sense of changing student needs and, by association, organizational strengths and weaknesses. In this way, systematic research and evaluation serve as signposts, helping to establish direction for student affairs organizations.

Observations about the Use of Research Findings

Using campus-based, decision-oriented research effectively in student affairs organizations requires practice. With practice comes the ability to choose research topics and methods that bear most directly on management and student development activities.

It should be noted well that "use" does not always imply direct action. Whereas instrumental use is documentable use of information to make a decision or solve a problem, conceptual use is the more abstract influence of research on thinking, whether or not action is taken. It is not always clear when each of these types of use occurs because the influence of information on an individual's thinking is difficult if not impossible to track.

Nevertheless, there have been some interesting efforts to assess organizational use of research. Weiss and Bucuvalas (1980) associated perceived usefulness of research with research quality, action orientation, conformity of user expectations, challenge to the status quo, and relevance (pp. 303-07). Similarly, Leviton and Hughes (cited in Cooley & Bickel, 1986) identified five clusters that seemed to be consistently related to use: relevance of the evaluation activity, communication between evaluators and potential users, information processing on the part of potential users, perceived credibility of the research product, and user involvement and advocacy (p. 124).

Weiss (1981) cautioned against making an arbitrary distinction between instrumental and conceptual use of research, suggesting that the use of research is actually a continuum wherein "research evidence is taken into account but does not drive the decision . . . users filter research evidence through their knowledge, judgment, and interests, and incorporate much besides research into decision making" (p. 23).

Based on their experience using student affairs research as a management tool for decision making at Syracuse University, Eickmann, Baigent, and Froh (1988) have observed that potential uses of data can be conceptualized as an awareness-action continuum. Observation and enlightenment comprise the "awareness" end of the continuum. Management, planning, and decision making are at the "action" end of the continuum.

Case study literature in student affairs is emerging that demonstrates a concern for the dissemination, use, and impact of campus-based research. Moxley (1988) described ways in which research findings are intentionally introduced into the decision-making environment at the University of Texas at Arlington:

> At the conclusion of each project, the findings are reviewed with the vice president and other interested parties (e.g., committee members if the research was conducted for a committee, the department director if the project was a program evaluation). In addition, a considerable number of the research reports are sent to student affairs staff members and all other administrative officials, including academic department heads. The reports typically contain a summary of findings accompanied by tabular data and, when appropriate, descriptive charts and graphs. To maintain the neutrality and objectivity of the office, interpretations of the data and recommendations are not included (p. 177).

Moxley (1988) also met with major stakeholders and decision makers to determine how specific research reports were being used. She found, for example, that reports on retention, together with information from withdrawing student surveys, had the following uses and impacts: (a) documented the effectiveness of Special Services (a federally supported program) and the college adjustment class for new students; (b) provided responses to information requests from external agencies (e.g., accreditation teams, state and federal agencies); (c) served as an impetus for developing an intrusive advisement program for minority students; (d) developed financial aid policy for continuing aid, given the student's academic progress; (e) mobilized student organizations to develop retention strategies; and (f) during student orientation, helped students to recognize factors that could retard their academic progress (p. 177). She determined that other reports ". . . increased employee efficiency and effectiveness, fostered changes in program implementation, prompted development of new programs, identified programs no longer in line with students' needs or interests, . . . answered questions required for decision making, helped curb spending, and encouraged planning" (p. 179).

At Home in Wonderland

In this monograph, allegorical references to Wonderland on the topic of student affairs research are more than whimsical. In a very real sense, each college and university in the American system of higher education is a unique environment ("curiouser and curiouser"), like Wonderland. No two institutional missions are exactly alike. No two student populations are the same. Faculties, sources of funding and support, physical plant, administrative structure, academic expectations, and educational processes and outcomes all differ from one institution to the next.

The elusive big picture—the essence of organizational and educational culture in each college Wonderland—is too complex to be captured in any one form of overview. Rather, it is necessary and useful to chip away at the puzzle to gain incremental, purposeful insights and understanding. College administrators must work at knowing their own institutions and the students who comprise them. Student affairs professionals will probably always persist in thinking and talking about how they can intervene to improve their organizations and to enhance student life within them. It should be clear by now that student affairs research and evaluation activities hold considerable promise for guiding the planning, policies, and decisions that will make such dreams reality.

References

Astin, A.W.; Green, K.C.; and Korn, W.S. (1987). *The American freshman: Twenty year trends, 1966–1985.* Los Angeles: Higher Education Research Institute, University of California.

Beeler, K.J.; Benedict, L.G.; and Weitzer, W.H. (1984). The role of student opinion surveys in campus problem solving. Paper presented at the Northeast Association for Institutional Research, Albany, New York.

Brown, R.D. (1986). Research: A frill or an obligation? *Journal of College Student Personnel, 27*(3), 195.

Carnegie Foundation for the Advancement of Teaching, The. (1987). *A classification of institutions of higher education.* Lawrenceville, N.J.: Princeton University Press.

Chickering, A.W. (1969). *Education and identity.* San Francisco: Jossey-Bass Publisher, Inc.

Cooley, W.W., and Bickel, W.E. (1986). *Decision-oriented educational research.* Boston: Kluwer-Nijhoff.

Eickmann, P.E.; Baigent, P.M.; and Froh, R.C. (1988). Using research and evaluation as a management tool for decision making. Unpublished manuscript, Syracuse University, Office of the Vice President for Student Affairs.

Hull, Jr., D.F.; Hunter, D.E.; and Kuh, G.D. (1983). Alternative perspectives on student affairs organizations. In G.D. Kuh (ed.), *Understanding student affairs organizations.* (New Directions for Student Services Monograph #23). San Francisco: Jossey-Bass Publisher, Inc.

Johnson, D.H., and Steele, B.H. (1984). A national survey of research activity and attitudes in student affairs divisions. *Journal of College Student Personnel,* 25(3), 200-05.

Kuh, G.D. (1983). Guiding assumptions about student affairs organizations. In G.D. Kuh (ed.), *Understanding student affairs organizations.* (New Directions for Student Services Monograph #23). San Francisco: Jossey-Bass Publisher, Inc.

Moxley, L.S. (1988). The role and impact of a student affairs research and evaluation office. *NASPA Journal,* 25(3), 174-79.

Stufflebeam, D.L. (1983). The CIPP model for program evaluation. In G.F. Madaus, M. Scriven, and D.L. Stufflebeam (eds.), *Evaluation models: Viewpoints on educational and human services evaluation.* Boston: Kluwer-Nijhoff.

Tyler, R.W. (1976). *Prospects for research and development in education.* Berkeley: McCutchan.

Weiss, C.H. (1981). Measuring the use of evaluation. In J.A. Ciarlo (ed.), *Utilizing evaluation* (pp. 17-33). Beverly Hills, Calif.: Sage.

Weiss, C.H., and Bucuvalas, M.J. (1980). *Social science research & decision making.* New York: Columbia University Press.

Chapter 2

In Search of the Lost Chord: Applying Research to Planning and Decision Making

Larry G. Benedict

The jury all wrote down on their slates, "She doesn't believe there's an atom of meaning in it," but none of them attempted to explain the paper.

"If there's no meaning in it," said the King, "that saves a world of trouble, you know, as we needn't try to find any. And yet I don't know," he went on, spreading the verses on his knee, and looking at them with one eye; "I seem to see some meaning in them after all . . . "

Alice's Adventures in Wonderland
Chapter XII: Alice's Experience

In Chapter One, the authors note that student affairs practitioners do not systematically use research and, in fact, may actively resist the use of it. They review some of the common complaints that practitioners make as being "too busy," or "it's too expensive." Finally, they argue for the profession to be more research oriented.

In some ways, this clarion call within the profession for improved practice based on research sounds about as realistic as providing homes for the homeless, saving the Brazilian rainforest, or achieving world peace. Everyone is talking about it but not many people are doing much about it. Respected people in the profession continue to advocate for the increased use of research, but it is still not widely practiced. Before one can make the case for expanded use of research, and see the practice become widespread, one needs to understand why practitioners avoid research.

Reasons for Failing to Conduct or Use Research

There are several significant reasons why practitioners do not systematically use research in their practice. Unless the profession understands these reasons and begins to address them directly, it is unlikely that the profession will ever be marked by wide use of research.

Williamson and Biggs (1975) explained that student affairs researchers "find it very difficult to make their research findings meaningful to those who make decisions in colleges or universities" (p. 290). Similarly, Johnson and Steele (1984) reported that student affairs research has little impact at the divisional or institutional level (p. 202). Recently Beeler and Oblander (1989), in a study of student affairs research activities in 570 American colleges and universities, found that research involvement is greatest in assessing the effectiveness of student affairs organizations (p. 9). A compelling case can be made that research activities in student affairs divisions are generally halfhearted, poorly planned, myopic, and ineffective.

Why do student affairs organizations fail to conduct and use meaningful research in their planning and decision making? To begin, attitudes toward research have been poor and are based on some misconceptions. Faced with a decision that needs objective input, decision makers too often make excuses to avoid putting time and energy into research. Matross (cited in Williamson & Biggs, 1975) described three research-inhibiting attitudes:

- research is too hard for me
- research is irrelevant
- research is something I don't care to do.

If these attitudes seem simplistic, there are at least four underlying conditions that make them more plausible:

- The language of research is too complex
- A myth exists that professionals are too busy to do research
- There is a common misconception that research is too expensive for limited budgets
- There is unnecessary confusion of roles caused by the use of such labels as "decision maker," "planner," and "evaluator."

Finding Meaning in the Use of Research

There are some steps student affairs practitioners can take to address these conditions. The profession needs to change or simplify the language of research, eliminate the myth of student affairs research as being too time consuming and expensive, better describe the decision-making process, and focus on the concept of improved practice. Until these things happen, like Alice, the profession will not see an atom of meaning in the use of research even though there are many, like the King, who do begin to see some meaning after all.

Simplifying the Language of Research

"I only took the regular course," said the Mock Turtle.
"What was that?" inquired Alice.
"Reeling and Writhing, of course, to begin with," the Mock Turtle replied; "and then the different branches of Arithmetic—Ambition, Distraction, Uglification and Derision."
"I never heard of 'Uglification,'" Alice ventured to say. "What is it?"

"Well then," the Gryphon went on, "if you don't know what to uglify is, you are a simpleton."
Alice did not feel encouraged to ask any more questions . . .
Alice's Adventures in Wonderland
Chapter IX: The Mock Turtle's Story

To most of us, confronting a foreign language can be intimidating, scary, confusing, and frustrating, just as Alice's experience in her discussion on learning with the Mock Turtle and the Gryphon. In that discussion Alice confronts many new terms, including "uglification," which she does not understand. Similarly, the language of research can be arcane, obscure, and unintelligible to ordinary mortals. For most students, the required course in research at the master's degree level addresses the language of research in a way that seems divorced from the everyday life of the practitioner. Terms and phrases like "quasi-experimental," "randomization," "control groups," "inferential statistics," "analysis of covariance," "canonical correlations," "multiple regression," and "beta weights" mean about as much to most student affairs professionals as "uglification" means to Alice. Like Alice, many professionals probably feel like "simpletons" when it comes to the language of research.

The language of the research methods course is that of the conclusion-oriented researcher, rather than that of the everyday practitioner or decision maker. It is the language of the experimental researcher and it is this language that can seem so scary and confusing. This language can be contrasted with decision-oriented research (Cronbach & Suppes, 1969). In their classic work, Cronbach and Suppes (1969) sought to understand why educational practice was not being affected by reason to a greater extent than was the case. To help the reader better understand the issue, they described two approaches and tried to explain how each influences educational practice. (See Chapter One for further discussion of decision-oriented research.) Conclusion-oriented research seeks to generalize about realities that apply in all or most settings. Decision-oriented research is more concerned with what works in a specific setting, seeking objectivity but limiting its focus to immediate situations.

How does this research notion apply in student affairs administration or student development theory? The answer lies in Chickering's reminder that " . . . in translating any general theory into concrete applications, the specifics of particular contexts, particular combinations of institutional mission, and student characteristics need to be taken into account" (Thomas & Chickering, 1984, p. 394). It is through such research that we gain an understanding of students, their needs, and appropriate planning alternatives at our individual campuses.

For example, the director of the new student program (NSP) is designing a new, overnight orientation program for incoming students. She wants to know what works in overnight programs for traditional-aged students in a metropolitan university. The director does not want or need to design an elaborate new program, randomly assigning some students to the new program, holding some students out as a control, pretesting both groups, making sure that none of the threats to internal and external validity has been violated, etc. One can readily see that faced with such a task, very few if any NSP directors would want to rush into the thicket.

However, the NSP director does want to provide the very best program for her students in her setting. This can be done with simple data collection techniques, in a timely and effective fashion. The data she needs to use in helping make these decisions could be simply gathered by calling some peer institutions which have similar programs. The director does not care if the program she is deciding upon is the best program in the country, or that it works at all universities, or that all traditional-age students in all settings benefit from the program. Rather, she wants to know what will work for her program, with her kinds of students at another institution.

It is this message that needs to be communicated to the practitioner. The language and methods of decision-oriented research need to be made widely and simply available to practitioners (Popham, 1975; Bogdan & Bicklen, 1982).

As noted, most practitioners have learned whatever research skills they may possess in a conclusion-oriented mode and, therefore, see no connection between those skills and their decision-oriented needs. If practitioners are not taught or do not understand the connection between research and practice, they will never systematically use research. Like Alice, they won't understand the Gryphons and Mock Turtles and will be condemned to wander about Wonderland discouraged about asking any more questions.

Research is Not Always Time Consuming

"Oh my ears and whiskers, how late it's getting!" said the White Rabbit hurrying down the long passage.

Alice's Adventures in Wonderland
Chapter I: Down the Rabbit-Hole

The fallacy that research is time consuming, perhaps better called an excuse, also stems from the confusion between conclusion-oriented and decision-oriented research. Carefully controlled experimental designs which seek to test hypotheses of universal significance can indeed be expensive. However, these designs go beyond what practitioners typically need. Practitioners need specific information that relates to immediate problems, concerns, and decisions.

Decision-oriented data collection need not be time consuming. Consider, for example, the health educator who must recommend within three days whether condom machines should be installed on campus. The health profession at large is clearly in favor of this program, but in the health educator's campus and community setting condom machines may not be well received. In fact, the administration has denied a request for such installation in the past.

The health educator wants to be on solid ground in dealing with this emotionally charged decision. To make the decision, this practitioner called 10 other universities with similar campus settings, some in similar communities, to see what they were doing; called several vendors to see what their experiences have been; and consulted the American College Health Association (ACHA). Based on this data collection, a decision was made about what to do (install the machines) and how and when to do it (through a coordinated, integrated health education program at the college). This was presented as a comprehensive proposal to the vice president and president who approved it. The program was successful.

This is an actual example. The total staff time required to make the telephone inquiries was perhaps an hour. The time to write the proposal and present it to the administration did not exceed three hours. This was not terribly time consuming even for very busy people. Furthermore, it worked.

Research Can be Cost-effective

Decision-oriented research need not be expensive, although it can be made expensive if enough resources are brought to bear. The myth that "we can't afford it" again stems from the misconception that all research designs are elaborate and time consuming. In the example of the condom machines cited above, total cost for the telephone calls was about $15 and the cost of copying the proposal was a few dollars. Even adding indirect costs such as staff time and electricity for the word processing, total costs here were no more than $50. This is not costly even on a shoestring budget.

This is also a good example of the obverse: sometimes an institution can't afford not to do the data collection, for political or educational reasons or because making the wrong decision will prove more costly in the long run. In the condom machine example just cited, an earlier attempt to install them had failed because a convincing case using data had not been made. The decision not to install was made based on a possible "morality" argument or the conventional wisdom on campus about the political climate. Without comparative data from other institutions and information from ACHA, the campus lost nearly two years of the benefits of this particular program.

Another example illustrates how data gathering prevented a potentially dangerous situation. The directors of residence life, police and safety, and health services at one university launched a fire safety prevention program in the residence halls. They decided to survey some residence hall students to see whether their efforts had been successful. The results of this data collection indicated

> that the students surveyed were woefully ill prepared to respond to a fire emergency despite brochures having been distributed, resident assistants and hall directors having informed students about procedures, and so on. In this case, the educational effort was not working and new programming was required. Such programming was developed immediately (Madson, Benedict & Weitzer, 1989, p. 519).

This example clearly illustrates the value of research in planning; it allows the decision maker to take a proactive stance and avoid a problem, rather than reacting to a disaster after it has occurred.

This research was also conducted with a telephone survey at moderate cost. Methods and costs of decision-oriented research are discussed in the next chapter. (See also Madson et. al., 1989, for further discussion of these issues.)

The Role of the Generalist Includes Research

The student affairs profession promotes the concept of "generalist" in describing the activities of the student affairs practitioner. Among the skills needed by generalists are the abilities to read, conduct, disseminate, and use research and evaluation. Unfortunately, the labels people used to describe themselves and others often determine how they and others behave. Using language like "decision maker," "planner," or "evaluator" in talking about the use of research can sometimes scare staff from even considering the systematic use of data to improve their decisions. Many student affairs staff do not use such labels to describe themselves, even though much of their activity falls into these functional areas.

Williamson and Biggs (1975) noted that "all student personnel workers can be researchers. Although many are not equipped with statistics or research methodology, they can adopt experimental and empirical attitudes as they deal with complex social behavior" (p. 295). This includes entry-level staff who may often think that department heads and vice presidents are the sole decision makers. Resident directors make decisions about the kinds of programs and activities to sponsor in their halls. Student activities staff make decisions about which events can be scheduled during the year and how much money can be spent on those events. The health educator makes decisions about materials to purchase for National Collegiate Alcohol Awareness Week.

These staff see themselves as "practitioners" rather than "decision makers" even though they continually make decisions. The profession needs to help staff understand that labels are secondary to the task of systematically improving professional practice. Within the profession, student affairs practitioners (generalists, specialists, whatever) need to stay abreast of current research and develop their own skills for gathering and using meaningful data. Only through practice does a practitioner become skillful in applying research to planning and decision making.

The Practitioner as Decision Maker

Student affairs staff do not usually view themselves as researchers, planners, or decision makers. They do view themselves as practitioners, and there is no question that they want to be the very best practitioners they can be.

As they practice delivering service to students, caring for students, supporting students, enhancing student development, and managing the cocurricular experience, student affairs staff continually, almost unconsciously, make decisions. These decisions number in the dozens per day, hundreds per month; perhaps thousands per year. No matter how centralized the organization, decision making is largely decentralized out of necessity.

Curiously, one often hears, "Oh, decision makers work above me on the organizational chart." This is simply not true. Everyone is a decision maker in the language of decision-oriented research, but many do not know it. The last time you bought a car, how did you do it? Did you test drive one or two? Did you read about selected models in an automobile magazine or consumer report? It is likely that you used one of these "research" strategies to gain useful information before making your purchase decision. How many readers have stopped smoking because of something they have heard or read about the effects of smoking? Is that oat bran muffin or oat bran cereal on your table there to reduce your cholesterol?

The point of these examples is that people base many, many decisions on information ("data" in the research language) gathered by themselves or others but don't consciously say, "I am using research results in making the decision to eat oat bran muffins." Student affairs practitioners do the same thing in their professional lives, often as easily as when they shop for a car, change their diets, buy a house, or choose a college to attend. One can describe the subconscious decision-making process:

1. A need or a problem arises: "I need a car."
2. Possible solutions require information: buy a car, lease a car.
3. Information is gathered: about cars, models, maintenance records, safety records, relative costs.
4. A decision is made: to buy a particular car.

Some decisions in our daily lives are made almost automatically, such as brushing one's teeth in the morning or checking the gas gauge prior to buying gasoline. Others are made very deliberately: which comedy team should be sponsored for Winter Carnival, or who will facilitate a workshop on AIDS. Deliberation, by nature, requires information which comes largely from some combination of four sources:

- Personal experience and intuition
- Experience of others: friends, peers, supervisor
- Authority: the literature, the president, Chickering, Astin's research
- Data gathered to describe or inform a specific problem: research

Each of these information sources is appropriate for certain decisions. For example, routine, daily decisions are probably best made using the first category: personal experience and intuition. This style is fast, comfortable, and easy to use. The drawback of this approach is that personal knowledge gained can be quite haphazard or limited, subject to selective memory, and isolated from the knowledge of others.

Relying on the experience of others is also useful in making relatively limited, ordinary, daily decisions. Knowing what other resident assistants (RAs) are doing to enforce quiet hours or how they are enforcing quiet hours can be very helpful for the RA who is looking for suggestions.

The third style, appealing to some external authority or expert can dramatically improve the deliberative decision-making process. For example, one might consult Astin's research and related literature to design programs to improve freshman retention. While this is a step in the right direction, it has some limitations as well:

- the data were gathered on students from all over the country and may not apply to the types of students at a particular institution
- the data interpretation may be biased in the direction of the belief and values of the researcher

- the method of collecting the data may be instructive, but the actual gathering of data must be duplicated or amended at the decision maker's own campus.

The fourth category, the one which is best described as data collection for decision making, is the one which is best suited for the nonroutine decisions which practitioners make. The health educator's decision on the condom machines and the new student program director's decisions about the overnight program are examples of nonroutine decisions to which data-gathering techniques should be applied. This style approaches the problem or decision systematically, asks what information is needed, and then determines how to gather that information. Clearly personal experience is involved to some extent, perhaps reliance on others as well. Often some regional or national information may be gathered. The difference is the focus on the immediate decision needed on a particular campus or in a specific campus setting.

Systematic use of appropriate information will lead to better, more efficient, more effective decisions. This will lead to better practice at all levels in the profession, which in turn becomes a self-perpetuating process when its value is noted.

To paraphrase Blanchard and Johnson (1982), people who produce good work feel good about themselves. People who feel good about themselves produce good work. Our work will be improved by the systematic use of data in our decision-making processes. This, in turn, will improve morale and productivity.

Examples of Decisions Informed by Research

To make this process of data collection and decision making more apparent, it is useful to take a closer look at examples used by the student affairs "researcher" operating behind the mask of "practitioner." The following are actual examples where practitioners have systematically gathered data to inform their decisions. Each decision was effective. All of these "research studies" were done at low cost within a relatively fast time frame. Each "decision maker" felt good about the results of the research which resulted in better service to students and to the respective college or university. These examples are meant to be illustrative and are, therefore, not cluttered with specific details about methods, costs, and procedures.

Health Educator

The university does not have an AIDS policy. It needs to develop one. What should it contain? How should it be developed? How should it be disseminated? Data were gathered and analyzed. A policy was drafted, reviewed by the university's attorney, and adopted.

A new state law requires all entering students to be immunized. The problem is how to implement the law on campus and get students to comply. Data from two similar universities were sufficient to develop procedures to bring the university into compliance with state law.

Orientation Director

A new program for traditional-aged students, including an overnight component, has just been implemented for the first time. Two major changes also included a new role for faculty advisors and a component for parents. Were these changes successful? Data gathered from the faculty indicate that while they liked the new design and felt it was more effective than the prior program, they would like additional training on working with the students in a one-on-one setting. This component will be revised to respond to this need. The parent data indicate there was too much unscheduled time during the first part of the program and that they would like more student interaction. This will be added to the program next year.

Director of Residence Life

The university has four different ID cards: one each for housing, food, the gym, and the library. Food Services is changing the way students are billed and the number of meal options available. This will require new technology which will make the current food ID inoperable. The director of residence life needs to address this change. As a result of his research, a new system was adopted which met the needs of all these constituents. The university will move to one ID card.

Director of Counseling

The director needs to balance the demand for services with staff resources available. The demand for career services has been escalating. The career counseling staff are overwhelmed. The director asks the vice president for more staff. The vice president suggests that the director survey students about their opinions/needs for career counseling services. One result of the study was that a majority of students reported they would prefer initial career counseling in group sessions rather than one-on-one sessions, which was current practice. The director implemented this new mode of delivery. Students were satisfied and much time became available for the career counseling staff, who wcrc also plcascd with the new format. It was not necessary to add any new staff.

The counseling director faces the possible need to remove a student from campus because of a psychiatric emergency. However, the university does not have a policy for such a situation. It is a tricky situation fraught with both health and legal liability issues. As a result of very rapid research, a policy was developed which successfully addressed the legal and health issues.

Financial Aid Officer

The office staff have been getting complaints from departments on campus about not being able to hire enough work-study students because the wage bands are too low. After a study of the local job market, wage bands were adjusted to make the university more competitive as an employer.

Admissions Office Counselor

A university has a large number of nontraditional students but its application form (in use for many years) is primarily geared to traditional students, even asking for such inappropriate information as parent address or high school GPA. (This university's typical students are older and many are parents themselves.) The problem is how to develop such a form, what it should contain, and so on. A brief collection of data was used to meet this problem. A different application was designed for nontraditional students, making the university more responsive to the needs of this group.

Dean of Enrollment Management

In the face of a declining pool of 18-year-olds, the dean needs to know a variety of things to help plan the university's enrollment: data on enrollers and nonenrollers, retention, primary and secondary markets, feeder schools, the university's image, etc. This is an example of a very complex study or series of studies needed to formulate an enrollment management plan. While this became a timely process as well as a costly one, it resulted in the university's first enrollment management plan, which was adopted by the campus administration. It was also done at a substantial savings over hiring an external consultant or consulting firm.

These examples have been provided to show the variety of practitioners in student affairs who have used data to improve decisions. In all of the examples except the last one, the data were gathered quickly and inexpensively. In all cases, the policies, activities, and decisions which resulted were effective. Staff did not get hung up on the language of conclusion-oriented research and often did not even use the word research to describe what they did.

In effect, gathering data became a routine problem-solving/decision-making process for these staff. The staff were also pleased and proud of their decisions. This, in turn, should lead them to incorporate data in future decisions.

By avoiding the language of the conclusion-oriented researcher, by eliminating the myths about time and cost elements of research, by avoiding the need for and use of labels, and by focusing on the outcomes—improved decisions leading to improved practice—these staff have found meaning in research. Unlike Alice, they did not need to know what uglification and reeling and writhing were and they did not feel like simpletons. Like the King, they have seen some meaning after all.

References

Beeler, K.J., and Oblander, F.W. (1989). A study of student affairs research and evaluation activities in American colleges and universities. Unpublished report. Washington, D.C.: National Association of Student Personnel Administrators, Inc.

Blanchard, K., and Johnson, S. (1982). *The one-minute manager.* New York: William Moore.

Bogdan, R., and Bicklen, S. (1982). *Qualitative research in education: An introduction to theory and method.* Boston: Allyn and Bacon.

Cronbach, L.J., and Suppes, P. (eds.). (1969). *Research for tomorrow's schools: Disciplined inquiry for education.* London: MacMillan.

Johnson, D.H., and Steele, B.H. (1984). A national survey of research activity and attitudes in student affairs divisions. *Journal of College Student Personnel,* 25(3), 200-05.

Madson, D.L.; Benedict, L.G.; and Weitzer, W.H. (1989). Using information systems for decision making and planning. In U. Delworth, G.R. Hanson, and Associates (eds.), *Student services: A handbook for the profession.* Second edition. San Francisco: Jossey-Bass Publisher, Inc.

Popham, W.J. (1975). *Educational evaluation.* Englewood Cliffs, NJ: Prentice-Hall.

Thomas, R., and Chickering, A.W. (1984). Education and identity revisited. *Journal of College Student Personnel,* 25(5), 392-99.

Williamson, E.G., and Biggs, D.A. (1975). Student personnel research. In E.G. Williamson and D.A. Biggs (eds.), *Student personnel work: A program of developmental relationships* (pp. 289-308). New York: John Wiley and Sons, Inc.

Chapter 3

Of Puzzles and Pieces: Organizing and Directing a Campus-Based Research Agenda

William H. Weitzer and
Gary D. Malaney

"Who are you?" said the Caterpillar.
This was not an encouraging opening for a conversation. Alice replied, rather shyly, "I—I hardly know, Sir, just at present—at least I know who I was when I got up this morning, but I think I must have been changed several times since then."
"What do you mean by that?" said the Caterpillar, sternly. "Explain yourself!"

Alice's Adventures in Wonderland
Chapter V: Advice from a Caterpillar

"Who are you?" This is a question asked constantly of students by student affairs researchers. The answers change as the topic changes and as time passes. Just as Alice changes in the Wonderland environment, college students change during their stay in the postsecondary environment. Who the students are, or to put it another way, what they are thinking is crucial information that can be utilized by decision makers in student affairs as they develop policies affecting student life.

While the need to gather data about student life is hardly debatable, how an institution goes about this process varies. Within student affairs, data collection options vary from those described in the previous chapter, using a single professional staff member to more systematic approaches involving an independent student affairs research office. In some institutions, although not recommended by the authors, the institutional research office takes full responsibility for collecting all student-related data.

Postsecondary institutions not only organize their research efforts differently, but also display distinctive preferences in their procedures for capturing data. Regardless of organizational structure or data-gathering practices, any effort to collect data on students will benefit from a preconceived plan of action. This chapter provides a conceptual framework for the design of student affairs research at any institution. This guide focuses on two essential variables that need to be considered prior to conducting research: cost and level of expertise.

The Need for Student Affairs Research

The need for more research within student affairs has been discussed for years by many researchers (Netusil & Hallenbeck, 1975; Crafts & Bassis, 1976; Webb & Bloom, 1981; Beeler, Benedict & Weitzer, 1984). However, one of the most often cited studies (Johnson & Steele, 1984) found little evidence that student affairs divisions devote large resources to research. Johnson and Steele (1984) analyzed questionnaire responses from 100 four-year colleges and universities to ascertain the "extent, type, usefulness, and structure of research activity currently conducted by student affairs divisions" (p. 201), and while they found that the vast majority (85 percent) of divisions conducted research (p. 201), only a few (12 percent) had separate research offices for that function (p. 203).

The authors also noted that research on student affairs was actually a quite recent development. In 1957, Weitz (cited in Johnson & Steele, 1984) found that research activity consisted basically of record keeping in the offices of deans of students. In the past 30 years, research on all aspects of the lives of college students has exploded. Yet there is still little evidence (at least in the scholarly literature) that student affairs divisions have increased their resources spent on research activity. Beeler and Oblander (1989), analyzing survey responses from 570 liberal arts, comprehensive, and doctorate-granting institutions, found that campus-based research within student affairs divisions is conducted only to a moderate extent, and that these research activities tend to be decentralized (p. 24).

Two recent publications have provided some insight into the workings of student affairs offices. Moxley (1988) discussed the responsibilities and goals of the Student Affairs Research and Evaluation Office (SAREO) at the University of Texas at Arlington. She detailed 28 objectives toward which the office works in addressing its goals and mission. She also provided specific examples of recently completed projects and their associated uses by and impacts on the campus community. Moxley's overview, however, did not provide details on how these projects were completed.

Thurman and Malaney (1989), on the other hand, have provided technical detail on how a specific type of research—telephone interviewing—is conducted at the Student Affairs Research and Evaluation Office at the University of Massachusetts at Amherst. They also provided a brief history of the office and described the development of SAREO's telephone interviewing operation known as Project Pulse.

Neither of these articles attempted to describe what resources a student affairs division needs to conduct detailed research, or the many types of research that might be useful in planning, policies, and decision making. These issues are discussed below through the examination of several research methods that vary by overall cost and needed expertise. A similar approach was recently used to discuss the design and use of information systems for decision making and planning (Madson, Benedict & Weitzer, 1989).

A Conceptual Guide for Research

Madson et al. (1989) described a four-step process for planning the design of information systems, which can also be applied in planning a research project. Those steps are:

- clearly articulate the research questions
- determine if existing data resources are available to address the research questions or what new research method would be required to address the question
- develop cost estimates and locate resources for implementing the research activity
- locate persons with the appropriate expertise to manage the research activity.

A clear articulation of the research questions is not as simple as it sounds. Often, requests for research are vague or mask a hidden agenda to "prove" that a program is doing its job or needs more resources. It is important that the research questions be clarified from the outset, especially for those groups (stakeholders) that might be affected by the research. Clarity about the goals and intentions behind research relieves anxiety about the project and adds credibility to the end product. Also, if many programs or departments are requesting research, clear articulation of the research questions and goals allows the chief student affairs officer or a research committee to set priorities for the research agenda. Often, staff members do not realize they need specific information to make effective decisions. In such cases, a frank discussion of information needs would improve the decision-making process.

Once the research questions have been identified, the second step is to conduct an inventory of what is already known and can be readily applied to the question. For example, most institutions have data made available to them by the College Board or American College Testing (ACT), and many have years of data from the University of California-Los Angeles Cooperative Institutional Research Program (UCLA/CIRP) survey of entering freshmen. In addition, information may already be available in offices within student affairs (e.g., counseling center), outside student affairs (e.g., institutional research), or in academic departments (e.g., education, psychology, sociology, communications, and marketing).

After completing these first two steps, if it is clear that a particular set of research questions has priority and that existing information cannot adequately answer these questions, new research may be needed. The remainder of this chapter focuses on how to select the best research method, taking into consideration both cost and availability of expertise. Cost and expertise are frequently interrelated. Expertise is often needed first to develop realistic cost estimates of specific projects, and later to manage research projects to hold down costs.

Methods of Research by Levels of Expertise and Cost

Four research methods that require low levels of expertise are described below. They are presented in ascending order of cost, from low to high.

Interpreting Existing Reports. The first and lowest cost method of research is the interpretation of already completed reports that have been generated from a variety of sources, either on or off campus. Most offices within a student affairs division will have, or have access to, many reports which have been filed without review. For example, many institutions receive reports from the College Board's Admissions Testing Program or the American College Testing (ACT) program concerning the characteristics of their applicant pool. In addition, almost all institutions participate in the collection of data for the federal government's Higher Education General Information Survey (HEGIS), from which reports are issued for use by colleges and universities. It is a relatively low cost, low expertise activity to pull these reports off the shelf and examine their potential use in decision making.

Within the institution, there are often annual reports prepared for the president or board of trustees that are seldom used to their full potential as information resources for planning and decision making. By taking advantage of an existing, expensive data collection effort, the student affairs practitioner with a small investment of time can put valuable information to work. One caveat is in order: care must be taken in the interpretation of information produced by another office. Knowing when and how the data were collected is important.

Informal Discussion and Observation. One of the easiest ways to collect new data regarding students is simply to hold informal discussion groups with a few students. Any student affairs practitioner, working with a few staff who are knowledgeable in a given area, can invite a small group of students to discuss an issue over coffee and doughnuts. This approach was used recently at the University of Massachusetts at Amherst in seeking student reaction to a proposed change in the alcohol policy.

Simple observational techniques are often a useful means of gathering data. For instance, regarding the alcohol policy, the university administrators decided to declare a ban on alcohol at outdoor events. To gauge student reaction to the policy, administrators simply attended outdoor events to observe student behavior.

One advantage of the informal discussion and observation approaches is that the interactive nature of the collection of information allows for greater flexibility than other information systems that are predetermined (e.g., surveys or computerized records). Other clear advantages are the rapid turnaround in the collection of information (e.g., dropping in at a residence hall one evening) and the immediate utility of the information (no computer analysis is necessary) in decision making. One drawback is that this method invites criticism because the sample is small, the data are not "representative," or the information is primarily qualitative (which will not satisfy those with a statistical orientation).

Interpreting Comparative Studies. Another type of analysis of existing student data involves comparing studies among institutions. This might involve comparing existing reports from several institutions. At minimal cost, this type of study can provide valuable information about how students at different types of colleges or universities compare. There may be a need for a moderate level of expertise to evaluate the validity of the comparisons (i.e., whether the comparison groups are appropriately defined, or variables exist that invalidate the comparison). There are also benefits to learning about how other institutions handle problems, organize themselves, and allocate budgets. The danger here is that comparisons are always inexact and require some qualification ("at this institution they charge X dollars for this activity, but that fee also covers Y"). Therefore, comparison studies should be used to guide decision makers, not drive the decisions themselves.

Using External Surveys with External Analysis. A final method that requires little expertise within student affairs, but which is very costly, utilizes external organizations that provide complete survey services at a major cost to the client, but require virtually no expertise from the client. Such organizations might even be found on campus, which could hold some advantages for the student affairs division, but the services may be no less expensive than off-campus organizations. The student affairs division at the University of Connecticut, for example, sometimes uses the Institute for Social Inquiry to conduct student opinion polls by telephone. The institute is campus based and is able to provide technical survey services for the division at relatively low cost.

External survey organizations can do everything from the initial design of a survey instrument through data collection, data analysis, and report writing. Purchasing the entire service for one survey can be quite expensive—perhaps several thousand dollars—depending on the survey method and the size of the sample. This approach is recommended only for one-time projects or single, annual projects, and obviously only if campus-based expertise is not available.

While they are not survey organizations specifically, the Cooperative Institutional Research Program (CIRP), the College Board, and the American College Testing Program (ACT) have developed surveys and other data collection techniques that provide valuable information even for institutions that have no survey expertise on staff. These organizations provide data entry and initial data analysis for their surveys, and more detailed analysis can usually be purchased as well. The cost of participating in some of these studies, such as the annual survey of entering freshmen coordinated by CIRP, is relatively low for the institution. Often the organization itself funds all or much of the project, due to its interest in the data.

Moderate Levels of Expertise

Five methods that require moderate levels of expertise are presented below. They are discussed in ascending order.

Computer Analysis of Existing Data. With a small increase in resources and expertise, it is relatively easy to conduct more sophisticated computer analysis of existing data. Basically, this requires that a student affairs division have at least one person on staff or otherwise available who has some expertise with database analysis software packages such as SAS or SPSS. This person might be a graduate research assistant on a campus with graduate programs in education or the social sciences, or it could be a faculty member available part-time or a staff member available in the office of institutional research.

More sophisticated computer analysis often involves re-analyzing data after the initial project has been completed. The idea is to use existing data to study other hypotheses or conjectures. The way SAREO uses the UCLA/CIRP data is a good example. After the dataset and accompanying report on freshman characteristics is sent to the university, staff members in SAREO feed the electronic dataset to the main-frame computer, run further analysis of the data, and write a report based on the new information. The object is to provide more useful information to administrators.

SAREO is often asked to re-analyze the Project Pulse telephone survey data from a particular poll to see how a segment of the students responded on a specific issue. The survey reports produced by SAREO typically report only the frequencies of scores for the entire group. When someone wants to know, for example, how only on-campus residents responded, additional analyses have to be run. While this is clearly not elaborate computer analysis, it does enable interested parties to answer additional questions from the same data.

A more elaborate example, which occurs from time to time, is when students in research classes choose to write data analysis papers and need datasets to analyze. These students often ask SAREO about existing studies on topics related to their interests. The students are welcome to take a SAREO dataset on a floppy disk and analyze the data in order to write a paper based on the results. SAREO staff members also utilize the same procedure in writing papers for publication.

Trend Analysis. A more specialized form of data analysis is called trend analysis, or looking at data collected over several years. This type of analysis can be performed with both computerized system records ("our applicants have gone up X percent, acceptances down X percent, enrollees up X percent") or computerized survey data.

SAREO actually collects a variety of data to analyze trends over the years. For instance, every other year a telephone survey of students is conducted on their attitudes and opinions pertaining to drug and alcohol use. The director of the student health center uses each year's data to add to his ongoing trend analysis to view changes in student behavior.

Another example involves SAREO's annual mail-out survey of students' attitudes, opinions, and activities. SAREO has been conducting this survey for 15 years and trends are reported as each year's data are added. An advantage of this type of analysis is that although there are few noticeable changes in student data from year to year, changes are apparent over three- or four-year cycles. A caveat in trend analysis is to be cautious in speculating about the influences behind trends.

Content Analysis. Moving toward higher cost and greater expertise, the next type of research practice is content analysis, a little-used technique within student affairs. Simply stated, content analysis entails reviewing either written or verbal communication to thoroughly understand the text. Reviews and critiques have been used for centuries by historians and literary critics, but only recently has content analysis emerged as a research technique in its own right by applying scientific methods to documentary evidence (Holsti, 1969). Content analysis consists of reviewing communication content and classifying the content according to a set of categories. Quantification of the data derived from the process usually plays a major role in the analysis.

To help illustrate the procedure, one could imagine that students, faculty, or administrators are concerned with what appears to be a recurrent bias in a student newspaper. To determine if systematic bias is evident, one could employ content analysis. The researcher would establish the categories of interest and count occurrences over an established time period with an appropriate sample of issues or stories. While the scientific approach of content analysis is almost never used in student affairs research, a more informal means of content review is often conducted whenever administrators read campus publications to better understand the environment.

Focus Groups. Still moving up the cost dimension but requiring only moderate levels of expertise, the next research practice is the use of focus groups. The cost of this practice can greatly vary, depending on whether one needs to hire a trained moderator or pay for a facility, or whether group participants must be paid. Since students generally are willing to participate at low cost, and a trained moderator and facility are likely to be available on campus, this research practice has been included as a moderate cost.

Focus group research basically consists of gathering a small number of subjects and a moderator to discuss a specific topic. Unlike the informal discussion sessions previously mentioned as a low cost, low-expertise method, the focus group incorporates several guidelines and controls. Welch (1985) suggested an optimum number of ten subjects and a discussion period of one to two hours. Subjects are chosen on the basis of their interest or experience in the topic and/or selected demographic characteristics. A trained moderator and a recording of the session are also strongly suggested.

Focus groups are primarily used in marketing research, and the use of focus groups in student affairs and higher education research has been negligible (Bers, 1987, 1989; Barrows & Malaney, in press). However, colleges and universities are undertaking more marketing-oriented research today as recruiting takes on increased significance; and for this type of research, focus groups are ideal.

For instance, Barrows and Malaney (in press) recently detailed a focus group study conducted by SAREO which investigated students' perceptions of the university's image and its promotional brochure. Sixteen undergraduate students and two moderators met for two hours and discussed a variety of issues, including academics, advising, social life, cultural diversity, university policies, and students' reasons for attending the university. The focus group proved to be very helpful in providing feedback to administrators by documenting the nature of the university's image problems.

The session also highlighted many problems that administrators have known about for years. As a result, administrators have made plans to address some of those problems.

External Surveys with In-House Analysis. This moderate-expertise, moderate-cost method involves using a survey research organization to design and administer a survey, then conducting the data analysis in house. While survey design expertise may not be available or may be difficult to find within the division, data entry and data analysis expertise should be much easier to locate in house. On campuses with graduate programs in the social sciences, there are probably dozens of graduate students who are both knowledgeable and available. Small colleges, again, might make use of faculty or staff in the institutional research office.

As mentioned before in the discussion of external survey organizations, this approach is fine for a student affairs division that is not interested in a great deal of survey activity and, therefore, does not want to hire a survey expert on staff. Care should be taken not to underestimate the level of expertise required to enter and analyze the data.

While SAREO has complete survey expertise on staff, it actually uses a variation of this approach in one instance. In participating in the UCLA/CIRP project, SAREO purchases a fairly complete service from CIRP, then conducts further analysis on the data and writes a related report.

High Levels of Expertise

Once an institution is prepared to dedicate a higher level of expertise, there are several other types of research practice that can be implemented. The final five methods presented require high levels of expertise, and are discussed in ascending order.

Database Analysis. In many institutions, in-house database analysis from a student database stored on a mainframe computer can require a high level of expertise. To perform this type of work, the student affairs division needs a systems expert, someone who is capable of manipulating often complex data from many system files to obtain accurate answers to queries. Depending on how the computer files are structured at a given institution, one might have to access various data files such as admissions, financial aid, and registration.

A good example of this type of research is a retention study. Recently SAREO was asked to produce some retention data for a given cohort group, students who enrolled for the first time during fall 1982. The data requested were graduation rates and withdrawal reasons by ethnic status. Since the university's administrative computer center had already created a data file for limited research purposes, SAREO's systems programmer only had to select the particular variables and the specific cohort group in question from that one file. A more sophisticated retention study is now being discussed, one which would require access to other files such as financial aid to explore the impact of student funding on retention. This project will require more expertise to manipulate the other files.

Telephone Survey. More than anything else, SAREO is known for its high-expertise, low-cost telephone polling operation called Project Pulse. The operation was described recently in some detail by Thurman and Malaney (1989). They noted that Project Pulse was originally established in 1972 as a means of gathering data for administrators to use in policy making. Today, Project Pulse surveys are typically requested by administrators within the student affairs division to assess some program or service or to simply obtain a better understanding of student opinion on a particular issue. A SAREO staff member, in conjunction with departmental administrators, designs an appropriate survey. The surveys are regularly administered (ten per semester) to 300 to 500 randomly selected students during the academic year. Interviewers are work-study students who are selected and trained by SAREO administrators. The interviewers are paid $5.25 hourly and ordinarily work from 5:00 - 10:00 p.m. each Wednesday night. As a cost-saving device, interviewers use telephones and computers in offices throughout the administration building, an approach which calls for more administrative supervision but capitalizes on an already established resource.

A weekly telephone survey of students can cost as little as $750 per survey if expenses (e.g., a graduate assistant) are spread over several surveys. The benefits include an ability to accurately gauge student attitudes about specific issues or programs, a higher response rate than most other methods, and an ability to ask questions specifically geared to the institution. A potential problem is finding the necessary expertise to conduct this form of sophisticated social science research.

Project Pulse is administered by a computerized survey research software package installed on 20 microcomputers in the various offices used by the interviewers. Data are entered during the interview process through electronic questionnaires. The next day, the raw data are converted to a SAS-PC file and frequency results are available by the end of the day. This process provides nearly instantaneous results for a department.

Specific examples of this operation are almost endless. In the past 17 years, there have been over 200 Project Pulse telephone surveys conducted on virtually every imaginable topic. A sample of topics include the following: computer use, sexual attitudes, smoking attitudes, racism, sexual harassment, alcohol use, fire safety, AIDS, course registration, residence hall life, food services, recreation, and radio listenership.

Mail Surveys. To conduct all aspects of a major mail survey project in house is a fairly costly enterprise that requires a high level of expertise. Expenses include printing, postage, envelope stuffing, response tracking, data coding and entry, data analysis, and report production. At each stage of the project, skilled staff need to be experienced in handling issues such as anonymity versus confidentiality, response rates, and missing data. If done well, the individualized nature of such a survey can increase its value to the institution. Of course, comparisons with other institutions are virtually impossible when an institution designs its own questionnaire.

SAREO conducts one major mail-out survey to students every year. Known as the CYCLES survey, it consists of items intended to measure student opinion and attitudes about their academic and social experiences on campus. The current practice is to sample 3,300 active undergraduates, who receive an initial letter and survey and a follow-up postcard reminder in ten days. Respondents are tracked and nonrespondents are mailed another letter and survey about three weeks after the initial mailing. An optimal response rate with this practice is around 60 percent. Because high response rate is viewed as critical for mail surveys, many efforts to increase student participation have been tried by SAREO over the years (Lam, Malaney & Oteri, in press).

Another type of mail survey periodically conducted by SAREO is called the Student Affairs at Selected Institutions (SASI) study. These surveys collect data from a predetermined group of institutions that have been designated (by sharing certain criteria) as peer institutions of the University of Massachusetts at Amherst. The data collected usually relate to program initiatives, budgets, and staffing within student affairs departments such as admissions, financial aid, or the registrar. Through these studies, the student affairs divisions in each of the participating institutions can see how they compare to the other universities responding to the survey. These data can be utilized to lobby for more operational funds or increased staff support.

Formal Observation. There are certain types of social science research practices that require very high costs and levels of expertise. It can be argued that these types of practices provide the highest quality of data researchers can obtain, but because of the costs involved, they are also the least likely forms of research to be undertaken. As a point of fact, SAREO has yet to use these research methods because the costs are simply too high. The first of these to be discussed is the formal observation study.

Like most of the research practices discussed in this chapter, formal observation methods can vary greatly in actual costs required. Much of the cost is based on the length of time a researcher needs to remain in the field to collect data through observation. Some anthropologists spend years in the field with their subjects. The length of time that would be necessary to study a certain group of subjects would depend upon the research interests. Some researchers believe that a longer stay in the field will yield more accurate data.

There are basically two types of observational studies: participant and nonparticipant. In participant observation, the researcher is actually a member of the group being studied. In nonparticipant observation, the researcher is not a member. In either situation, the researcher's role as observer may or may not be known to the group members being studied.

Face-to-Face Interviews. In survey research, face-to-face interviews are by far the most time consuming and expensive to complete. Obviously, they usually involve travel time for the interviewers and time to locate the specific respondents. These types of interviews are assumed to be the most effective means of gathering accurate data. A researcher generally obtains a higher response rate and therefore has greater confidence that the sample studied is representative of the general population.

While face-to-face interviews may be quite useful in qualitative research when the researcher wants to interview only a few individuals to obtain in-depth answers, the cost of surveying 400 individuals to make representative claims about a larger population is usually prohibitive. Most researchers have opted for the lower response rates of mail and telephone interviews to save time and money.

Formal observation and face-to-face interviews are but two examples of "naturalistic inquiry," discussed at greater length in the next chapter by Kuh. He makes a compelling argument for greater use of naturalistic research methods in student affairs and gives examples of how naturalistic inquiry can be applied to developmental processes and the quality of student life.

Discussion

SAREO began with only one graduate student about 16 years ago. The office developed slowly, but funding and staff were increased as the importance of the research was realized by the entire student affairs division. Today, SAREO serves a dual role by conducting research and coordinating information systems for the student affairs division. It is staffed by a director, an associate director, an assistant director, two classified staff members, three graduate students, and about 20 undergraduate students.

As a student affairs division develops a comprehensive research office, there may be concerns voiced from other areas of the institution such as the institutional research office, if one exists. The argument might be made that the institutional research office has all the resources needed to conduct student affairs research. Although the development, implementation, and use of student affairs research practices must be known to the campus officials responsible for institutional research activities, ideally they will be kept separate. Time constraints, staff resources, and institutional priorities usually dictate that student life research and evaluation projects will not be undertaken by institutional research staff. Institutional research offices, by definition, give priority to reviewing, analyzing and reporting academic and budget information, and responding to frequent requests for information from external agencies. With these commitments, they typically do not have the time or the inclination to develop a comprehensive student affairs research agenda.

Clearly, most student affairs divisions cannot be expected to obtain overnight the funding and expertise to implement most of the research practices discussed in this chapter. If there is virtually no research expertise on staff, the obvious suggestion is to do what Alice finally did to enter Wonder-land—"start small." It is generally advisable to begin by conducting research that requires low costs and low levels of expertise.

A simple way to start is to hire one student research assistant and assign some priorities about what needs to be investigated. One of the first things the research assistant should do is read the literature associated with the various topics to be investigated. It may be wise to hire a student who is interested in higher education issues, perhaps a graduate student in that field of study or an undergraduate interested in pursuing graduate study in higher education or student affairs.

If there are scattered elements of research expertise within the division, it might be possible to pool these resources into a centralized research effort. SAREO is a separate department reporting to the office of the vice chancellor for student affairs, and as such, is quite central-ized in its approach. There are several good reasons for a centralized approach. For instance, centralization helps prohibit promotion, through research, of the self-interest of any one department. Because a centralized research office has no special ties to a program or project, it is easier to avoid bias in the research. Related to this point, it is important that a certain amount of autonomy be housed in the research office, meaning that the administrators in that office main-tain control of a research project.

Centralization also limits the redundancy and waste that occurs when various offices within the division are conduct-ing their own research. Centralization allows for sharing resources and expertise. It promotes work that builds on past research and evaluation efforts. It creates an environ-ment which more easily allows for maintaining a history or catalog of research activity.

Whether an institution is starting small or has already developed a moderate to large research agenda, there should be no doubt about the importance of addressing the

Caterpillar's question, "Who are you?" Knowing and understanding students in this era of scarce resources and high accountability is critical to developing effective student services. Student affairs professionals who learn to use research in support of their planning, policies, and decisions will be the best equipped to advocate for student affairs in the coming years.

References

Barrows, C.W., and Malaney, G.D. (in press). Using focus groups in the marketing of higher education. *Journal of Marketing for Higher Education.*

Beeler, K.J.; Benedict, L.G.; and Weitzer, W.H. (1984). The role of student opinion surveys in campus problem solving. Paper presented at the Northeast Association of Institutional Research annual conference.

Beeler, K.J., and Oblander, F.W. (1989). A study of student affairs research and evaluation activities in American colleges and universities. Unpublished report. Washington, D.C.: National Association of Student Personnel Administrators.

Bers, T.H. (1987). Exploring institutional images through focus group interviews. *New Directions for Institutional Research,* 14, 19-29.

Bers, T.H. (1989). The popularity and problems of focus-group research. *College and University,* 64, 260-68.

Crafts, Jr., R.C., and Bassis, M.S. (1976). The university opinion index: Collecting student opinion quickly, accurately. *NASPA Journal,* 14(2), 59-61.

Holsti, O.R. (1969). *Content analysis for the social sciences and humanities.* Reading, MA: Addison-Wesley.

Johnson, D.H., and Steele, B.H. (1984). A national survey of research activity and attitudes in student affairs divisions. *Journal of College Student Personnel,* 25(3), 200-05.

Lam, J.A.; Malaney, G.D.; and Oteri, L.A. (in press). Strategies to increase student response rates to mail surveys. *Journal of Marketing for Higher Education.*

Madson, D.L.; Benedict, L.G.; and Weitzer, W.H. (1989). Using information systems for decision making and planning. In U. Delworth and G.R. Hanson (eds.), *Student services: A handbook for the profession.* (2nd edition). San Francisco: Jossey-Bass Publisher, Inc.

Moxley, L.S. (1988). The role and impact of a student affairs research and evaluation office. *NASPA Journal,* 25(3), 174-79.

Netusil, A.J., and Hallenbeck, D.A. (1975). Assessing perceptions of college student satisfaction. *NASPA Journal,* 12(4), 263-68.

Thurman, Q., and Malaney, G.D. (1989). Surveying students as a means of assessing and changing policies and practices of student affairs programs. *NASPA Journal,* 27(2), 101-07.

Webb, E.M., and Bloom, A. (1981). Taking the student pulse. *NASPA Journal,* 18(3), 25-30.

Welch, J.L. (1985). Researching marketing problems and opportunities with focus groups. *Industrial Marketing Management,* 14, 245-53.

Chapter 4

Rethinking Research in Student Affairs

George D. Kuh

"I could tell you my adventures—beginning from this morning," said Alice a little timidly: "but it's no use going back to yesterday, because I was a different person then."
  "Explain all that," said the Mock Turtle.
  "No, no! The adventures first," said the Gryphon in an impatient tone: "explanations take such a dreadful time."
Alice's Adventures in Wonderland
Chapter X: The Lobster Quadrille

Explanations can be tedious. To explain why a person enters a particular vocation, or what circumstances lead to the founding of a college, or why research methods in student affairs are changing, requires more than a little patience. The adventure of student affairs research over the past two decades is reflected in changing assumptions about how we come to know what we know and the methods we use to understand the behavior of students, faculty members, and others. Because this has been a silent revolution (Kuh, Whitt & Shedd, 1987; Schwartz & Ogilvy, 1979), the changes underway are not necessarily self-evident; thus, to paraphrase the Mock Turtle, some explaining is needed.

In the preceding chapter, Weitzer and Malaney described various approaches to student affairs research, based on assumptions about cost and expertise. They offered useful guidelines for developing cost-effective studies using, for the most part, conventional data collection techniques. This chapter challenges the student affairs profession to acknowledge some of the limitations of conventional research, and to embrace interpretive forms of inquiry that hold promise for richer understandings of students and student affairs work.

There are alternative approaches to inquiry variously called naturalistic (Lincoln & Guba, 1985), qualitative (Fetterman, 1988), ethnographic (Goetz & LeCompte, 1984), or appreciative (Cooperrider & Srivasta, 1987). However, in this chapter all these methods are called naturalistic because they seek data in the form of words, the meaning of the data is context bound, and, in so far as is possible, data are interpreted within the frame of reference of those who participate in the study. In this sense, the term naturalistic takes on a more comprehensive meaning than implied by Lincoln and Guba (1985).

The Warrant for Alternative Approaches to Student Affairs Research

Much of what is reported in the student affairs literature does not stimulate practitioners' imaginations nor accurately describe college and university life or the college student experience (Kuh, Bean, Bradley & Coomes, 1986). This discouraging state of affairs, however, is not limited to student affairs research (Keller, 1986). In Keller's (1985) words, "Hardly anyone in higher education pays attention to the research and scholarship about higher education" (p. 7). Important research is stymied by

> the notion that colleges and universities can be and should be studied scientifically . . . that social phenomena can be explained by "law-like generalizations" which derive from controlled, rigorous experiments in mathematical analysis, that social research can result in replicative situations and can provide predictive power for future events . . . (Keller, 1985, pp. 9-10).

Empirical descriptions of student affairs organizations, for example, are grounded primarily in conventional assumptions about organizing (Kuh, 1983) and reinforce expectations for control, linear causality, and tight coupling that contradict the experiences of student affairs staff (Kuh, 1989).

Lincoln (1986) advanced five propositions that challenge the use of conventional inquiry approaches to understand higher education:

> (a) The social world in which we live is a construction, agreed to and enacted by us each day . . . (b) Pluralism and value conflicts characterize higher education more today than ever before. This pluralism and conflict will continue to dominate what we do . . . (c) Despite their historical heritages, our institutions of higher education are entirely new cultural, social, and human organizational forms—at least some of them—than have existed in the past . . . (d) The study of higher education is, in both historical and sociological terms, a "new" discipline . . . (e) The social sciences have literally locked themselves into a unitary way of knowing— that is, into one paradigm and one set of (primarily quantitative) methodologies" (pp. 136-37).

Student affairs professionals respond to the needs of diverse students in increasingly complicated college environments. Even the most sophisticated questionnaires or checklists designed to assess student or staff satisfaction are limited in their capacity to adequately capture certain experiences, such as the contributions made by a staff member who sits all night with a depressed student or who meets over the noon hour with a student government officer anxious about leading his or her first meeting. Are there other ways of generating information about student affairs work and the college student experience that will be more interesting and useful? Absolutely. Before entertaining these ideas, however, the characteristics of conventional research methods are briefly summarized.

The Conventional Approach to Research in Student Affairs

"Speak English!" said the Eaglet. "I don't know the meaning of half those long words, and what's more, I don't believe you do either!" And the Eaglet bent down its head to hide his smile; some of the other birds tittered audibly.

Alice's Adventures in Wonderland
Chapter III: A Caucus-Race and a Long Tale

The research models that dominate inquiry in student affairs were adopted from the physical sciences which assumed that (a) all relevant variables can be measured objectively, and (b) all physical events are determined by preceding events (Kuh, Whitt & Shedd, 1987). In the conventional inquiry paradigm, student affairs researchers assume they can objectively assess the phenomena under study and, through deductive analysis, determine the degree to which the "intervention" (e.g., meeting with a career counselor) "causes" or produces the desired outcome (e.g., a greater degree of vocational maturity). Thus, studies based on conventional inquiry assumptions (i.e., logical positivism) hold that there is a single reality and, through the use of a priori research designs and a sophisticated, time-honored set of rules (e.g., sampling that produces a "normal" distribution of people from a given population), the "truth" about the topic under investigation (e.g., the influence of career planning workshops on vocational maturity) can be discovered. In addition, the rules of conventional inquiry methods assume that if an intervention is carefully replicated in other settings, similar effects can be produced with students similar to those who participated in the original study (Campbell & Stanley, 1963).

However, many of the rules and assumptions on which conventional research is based are regularly violated (e.g., the sampling procedure does not produce a normal distribution of "subjects"). In addition, the sources and amount of statistical error are often underestimated, including insufficient internal validity such as failure to control all relevant variables, deficient external validity such as failure to use a representative random sample or obtain a high response rate, and measurement error such as measuring instruments that have low reliability and validity.

Postpositivism: Challenges to Conventional Research

Most physical scientists have discarded the belief that the physical universe is like a giant, predetermined clock (Capra, 1983). The Newtonian view that seemingly unpredictable phenomena, such as the formation and movement of clouds, are ultimately predictable has been challenged by a competing view that physical phenomena are in essence as unpredictable as clouds (Popper, 1979). For example, chaos theory, by embracing the paradoxical processes of determinism and indeterminism, has provided startling new insights into the behavior of physical phenomena, from dripping faucets to weather systems (Gleick, 1987). Briefly, chaos theory holds that although a strict deterministic causality operates at each individual step in an unfolding process, it is impossible to predict the outcome over any sequence of steps in the process (Maruyama, 1976). That is, even though relationships between variables can be characterized by simple deterministic laws, the outcome is completely unpredictable, even with the most precise available knowledge of the relevant initial conditions (Cziko, 1989). Furthermore, the nonlinearity and iterative nature of chaotic systems creates slight variations in early actions and behaviors that ultimately lead to large, unpredictable differences later. This ultrasensitive dependence on initial conditions, the "butterfly effect," was first made widely known by Lorenz (1963), who explained how the flap of a butterfly's wings in Brazil might trigger a tornado in Texas (Lorenz, 1979).

Although relatively unknown by most social and behavioral scientists, chaos theory is of considerable interest to physicists, mathematicians, biologists, astronomers, and economists (Prigogine & Stengers, 1984). Chaos may also have useful implications for understanding human behavior because it suggests that even though the relationship between two variables may be simple and deterministic, the relationship may result in outcomes that are entirely unpredictable. The unpredictability of human behavior partially explains why conventional student affairs research has not been as useful as research in the physical sciences. That is, we "have not been able to discover generalizations that are reliable enough, and about which there is enough professional consensus, to form the basis for social policy" (Phillips, 1980, p. 17).

The implications of indeterminacy and chaos for student affairs research are far-reaching. Comprehensive and definitive experiments are not possible; that is, student affairs researchers cannot realistically achieve prediction and control but rather only temporary understanding (Cronbach, 1975, 1982; Cronbach & Snow, 1977; Snow, 1977). For example, student development theory is based on the proposition that human development is continuous, patterned, orderly, predictable, and cumulative. This proposition leads to the possibility that human development can be intentionally facilitated; that is, programs can be developed to encourage students to "change" or "develop" in a manner consistent with the theories. Similar assumptions about order, patterning, rationality, and intentionality influence student affairs professionals' thinking and behavior with regard to planning, goal setting, and performance evaluation (Kuh, Whitt & Shedd, 1987). Such assumptions are no longer tenable in a world characterized by indeterminacy and uncertainty. Kuh, Whitt and Shedd (1987) discussed these issues in some detail (see also Caple, 1985, 1987; Howard, 1985; Lucas, 1985).

Naturalistic Inquiry Assumptions and Methods

It sounded like an excellent plan, no doubt, and very neatly and simply arranged; the only difficulty was, that [Alice] had not the smallest idea how to set about it. . .

Alice's Adventures in Wonderland
Chapter IV: The Rabbit Sends in a Little Bill

Every observation is filtered through the observer's belief system, or personal theory of the world. As the physicist Jeremy Hayward put it, "I'll see it when I believe" or conversely, "I won't see it because I don't believe" (cited in Cooperrider & Srivastva, 1987, p. 167), If human experience is—in essence—symbolically represented in the minds of people, human development, organizational behavior, and the college experience may be better conceived of as unfolding dramas of human interaction (Cooperrider & Srivastva, 1987).

By challenging explanations rooted in logical positivism, the "silent revolution" mentioned earlier is the harbinger of an interpretive form of inquiry that describes activities and events in the context in which they occur. This approach to research is "looking less for the sorts of things that connect planets and pendulums and more for the sorts that connect chrysanthemums and swords" (Geertz, 1980, p. 165). Instead of "certainty through science," researchers in all fields are now embracing inquiry approaches that emphasize history, the behavioral context, and ever-changing interpretative schemes used by members of a group to give life and meaning to their actions and decisions (Bartunek, 1984). Examples of such research include Clark's (1970) work on the importance of the organizational saga for understanding how faculty members and administrators use the past to interpret current events and Tierney's (in press) study of the influence of institutional culture on curriculum reform. The assumptions and methods characteristic of naturalistic inquiry include the following.

Assumptions

1. Naturalism accepts—indeed embraces—multiple realities, not a single reality. Knowing is acknowledged to be an act of interpretation and individuals lend their own interpretation to events and actions, including their own behavior.

2. Knowledge and the meaning made of data are idiographic and context bound. That is, what is discovered cannot be understood out of the context in which the data have been gathered. Also, knowledge cannot be generalized to other settings and people.

3. Behavior is indeterminate, not predictable or controllable. Change in attitudes, behavior, and institutional policies and practices occurs through evolutionary, mutual shaping between environments and people. Neither the environment nor human behavior are predictable or open to direct control.

4. Words and symbols as data lead to richer, more complicated understandings of college and university life than can be obtained by pencil and paper instruments that predetermine, and thus constrain, participants' responses, such as questionnaire surveys using Likert scales.

Methods

1. Flexible, responsive research methods are required. Because human behavior is unpredictable, an investigator must be comfortable with the likelihood that research methods designed a priori tend to ignore what is discovered as the research process unfolds. Naturalistic researchers are free to pursue promising areas of understanding suggested by the data and participants. Also, as a study evolves, the pool of participants must be expanded to enrich understanding. Sampling techniques known as snowball sampling and status sampling (Dobbert, 1984) are often used. Snowball sampling suggests that participants be asked to identify others whose opinions or experiences are, based upon their knowledge, different from their own. Status sampling en-

sures that respondents are selected to represent important perspectives (e.g., administration—president, chief student affairs officer; students—student leaders, students of color; and faculty members—full time, part time, men, women).

2. The investigator is a human instrument, both observing and influencing that which is observed. Naturalistic methodologies generate "thick descriptions" (Geertz, 1973)—dense, in-depth interpretations of the underlying constructs that influence an outcome such as an individual's decision to go on to college. Participants, such as students and faculty members, are encouraged to use their own language rather than the terms imposed or preferred by the investigator.

3. Interviews and observations are primary modes of data collection, as they enable the researcher to record the multiple meanings participants make of their experience. Individual interviews and focus groups are frequently used to gather data. Focus groups (Merton, Fisk & Kendall, 1956) are discussion groups that meet only once and concentrate on a specific topic, such as the value of holding a student government position. The degree of structure imposed on interviews may vary from less to more as an investigation proceeds and the researcher begins to learn more about the phenomenon under study.

4. Inductive analysis is used which allows the researcher to move from specific data obtained from individuals to general understanding. Participants are asked to verify interpretations made by investigators, thus correcting and enriching investigators' interpretations of actions and events. Data analysis and data collection occur simultaneously; thus, data analysis informs data gathering. One example of inductive data analysis is Glaser and Strauss' (1967) constant comparative method: (a) identifying units of data, (b) using units of data to develop categories, (c) comparing incidents or observations applicable to each category, (d) integrating categories and their properties, (e) delimiting the theory, and (f) writing the theory.

5. The investigator and participants or respondents (the term *subject* is never used!) collaborate throughout the inquiry process. The collaborator "researcher-researched relationship" should be built on mutual respect, dignity, honesty, and trust (Skrtic, 1985) which allow reciprocity—a give and take, a mutual negotiation of meaning and power (Lather, 1986). Reinharz (1978) described this relationship as a "lover model," denoting equality and respect, rather than a "rape model," common to conventional approaches in which the researcher takes what she or he wants and leaves. The negotiation process between the inquirer and participants must be clearly stipulated, however, because participants sometimes wish to "unsay" their words (Lather, 1986). A wise course of action is to permit participants "the right to comment" (Tripp, 1983, p. 39). In this sense, the researcher is more like a majority shareholder (rather than the owner of the data) who must justify decisions and give participants a public forum for critique (Lather, 1986).

Ensuring the Quality of Naturalistic Research

Naturalistic research is more complicated and rigorous than merely asking a few people what they think. The critical test is whether "the findings of an inquiry are [trustworthy], worth paying attention to, worth taking an account of" (Lincoln & Guba, 1985, p. 290). The criteria for trustworthiness include credibility (i.e., the investigator's constructions are credible to the respondents), transferability (i.e., the study may be useful in another conext), dependability (i.e., the reporting of results considers possible changes over time), and confirmability (i.e., the data can be confirmed by someone other than the inquirer). When possible, the investigator can enhance the credibility of his or her findings by conducting debriefings with other members of the research team or a peer debriefer, someone familiar with qualitative inquiry methods and the phenomenon being studied (Miles & Huberman, 1984). Debriefings are used to test ideas, obtain feedback on methods such as interview techniques, and to discuss next steps.

Member checks, another required step, are debriefing sessions with participants to test the data, interpretations, and conclusions and to judge the overall credibility of the findings (Lincoln & Guba, 1985). At the end of an interview, an investigator may review with participants what he or she has heard and seek feedback and clarification of the investigator's interpretations. Also, it is recommended that information be recycled among participants through an oral debriefing at the end of a round of data collection or through a written case report. For a fuller treatment by which the criteria of trustworthiness can be established, consult Lincoln and Guba (1985).

A Glimpse of Student Affairs Research in the Future

Alice said nothing; she sat down with her face in her hands, wondering if anything would ever happen in a natural way again.

Alice's Adventures in Wonderland
Chapter X: The Lobster-Quadrille

Research in the social sciences is moving inexorably from a conventional, positivist research paradigm that values prediction and control, to approaches that acknowledge the contributions of conventional research but also embrace and value attempts to describe, understand, interpret, and appreciate collective and individual behavior. Curiously, although the student affairs field is based on the premises that each person is unique and that individual differences should be celebrated, the inquiry methods used in the majority of papers published in student affairs journals are grounded in the positivist inquiry paradigm which masks institutional as well as individual differences (Kuh, Bean, Bradley & Coomes, 1986). The student affairs field has certain traditions that are quite compatible with naturalistic inquiry, such as becoming engaged—both intellectually and emotionally—in students' development and individual and group decision making. The act of engagement surely influences what students and student affairs staff experience and how they experience it. Thus, it makes sense that engagement also characterize the inquiry process in student affairs (Kuh, Whitt & Shedd, 1987).

In the future, the student affairs field can expect that an increasing number of studies will emphasize description and understanding, using units of analysis varying from macro level (e.g., campus, residence hall or fraternity house) to the micro level (e.g., behaviors, feelings, developmental processes of individual students). At the macro level, descriptions and interpretations of institutional cultures and subcultures, both familiar (e.g., Greek organizations) and less familiar (e.g., collectives of people of color), will be needed.

Naturalistic studies of educational policies, practices, behaviors, and outcomes are also needed to better understand and appreciate the complexity of higher education, student diversity, and to suggest what is possible and what may not be possible. More important, such research will provide ideas for innovations, a crucial source of variation needed for colleges and universities to evolve in creative ways (Clark, 1984). Case studies (Yin, 1984) will probably be used more frequently because they approximate "the natural experience" (Stake, 1978, p. 5). However, because case studies usually produce complicated descriptions of events and behavior, they also generate more for researchers and practitioners to pay attention to rather than less.

At the micro or individual student level, descriptive studies could be conducted to improve the understanding of social adjustment and problem-solving processes. An excellent example is Attinasi's (1989) study of the persistence of first-year Mexican American university students. Attinasi inductively analyzed in-depth, open-ended interviews and generated hypotheses about the sociopsychological context of this understudied student group. As with other naturalistic studies, Attinasi's research does not allow hard and fast predictions of human behavior or the design of "cook-book" solutions to problems faced by Mexican American students because of the complicating factors of individual differences, chaos, the evolutionary nature of learning and development, and the role of free will in shaping human behavior. As Cziko (1989) argued, "It is a serious error to believe that one can predict the future based on what has happened in the past" (p. 23). Thus, qualitative inquiries into pressing issues facing the student affairs field may produce important information about the possible, but cannot point to what is necessary or inevitable (Cziko, 1989).

Applications of Naturalistic Inquiry Methods

And the moral of that is—"be what you would seem to be"— or, if you'd like to put it more simply—"never imagine your-self not to be otherwise than what it might appear to others that what you were or might have been was not otherwise than what you had been would have appeared to them to be otherwise."

Alice's Adventures in Wonderland
Chapter IX: The Mock Turtle's Story

Kuh, Whitt and Shedd (1987) discussed some applications of naturalistic research to issues related to the quality of student life and developmental processes during the college years. In this section, three critical issues facing the field are used to illustrate how naturalistic inquiry methods can be used to better understand matters about which student af-fairs professionals need and want to know more.

The Impact of Student Life Policies

Relatively little is known about how student life policies and practices influence the quality of the undergraduate experi-ence. Of course, the relationships between policies, prac-tices, and student behavior are context bound, a sine qua non, of naturalistic inquiry. Thus, campus-specific studies of the relationship of student life policies to student development are required. To determine, for example, whether the student organization resource allocation process is having the desired effect, such as encouraging student involvement in activities compatible with the educational purposes of the institution, a systematic analysis could be made of characteristics and motivations of members of various student groups who participate in the resource allocation process, and the availability of resources to encourage formation of new groups. A team of student life staff members, faculty members, and students could interview student leaders, observe the resource allocation process, and attempt to understand why some groups are successful in obtaining funds while others are not, and whether the activities of funded organizations are compatible with the educational purposes of the institution. Useful data sources would include a historical analysis of funding patterns, the amount of resources available to student groups, both established and emerging, and a careful examination of the extent to which the activities of student organization members are compatible with the institution's educational purposes. Equally important is the extent to which the allocation committee "puts its money where its mind is." That is, is the resource allocation process open, democratic, and consistent with the education mission (Kuh, Schuh, Whitt, Andreas, Lyons, Strange, Krehbiel & MacKay, 1991)?

As noted earlier, to establish the trustworthiness of naturalistic research, written and oral interpretations of the allocation process must be shared, and comments must be received from those who participate in, or who are affected by, the policy and/or procedures. In one sense, the findings themselves may not be as important as the process the inquiry team uses to understand how resources are used to support student activities. That is, by interacting with various members of the campus community, the degree to which student activities complement the educational purposes of the institution will be better understood by many groups, including those persons who participated in the study.

Creating Affirming Campus Environments for Students of Color

The literature is unequivocal: most students of color find predominantly white institutions of higher education inhospitable (Fleming, 1984; Steele, 1989; Terrell & Wright, 1988). Of course, there are no quick fixes to the obstacles encountered by students of color. Nothing short of institutional transformations will be required to modify the policies and practices that alienate students of color, engender suspicion and dissatisfaction, and create obstacles to achievement and persistence (Kuh, 1990). This is a complicated issue, one that cannot be better understood using pencil and paper checklists.

Naturalistic methods can produce richer descriptions and understandings of both the diversity of student characteristics and the plurality of views, feelings, and interpretations represented by old and young students, students of color, and other groups. Naturalistic methods can also be used to identify institutional factors, conditions, and strategies that promote the success of students of color. Questions to be answered include: Why do students of color decide to go on to college? What are their experiences once enrolled? Why do some persist to graduation? Why do others leave before attaining their educational aspiration? What institutional policies and practices are related to their persistence?

Institutional change is almost always prompted by factors and conditions in the external environment (Sanford, 1962). Thus, external resource teams may be required to collaborate with institutional researchers to identify policies and practices and properties of the institutional culture that alienate students of color and other underrepresented groups. The purposes of institutional site visits are to assess the quality of the faculty and student experience at the institution and to identify institutional conditions that require attention to improve the satisfaction and achievement of students of color. External teams might make a series of site visits to an institution and conduct extensive interviews of students of color (on some campuses, virtually all students of color could be interviewed in a two-day period), student leaders, other students, faculty and administrators of color, other faculty and administrators, student affairs professionals, and community leaders.

The external resource team would share their findings with their counterparts on the institution-based team. Then, in collaboration with the team and other institutional agents and students, they would assist in determining how to best mobilize resources, develop intervention strategies (e.g., faculty development programs, coordination of enrollment management activities, modifications in student life policies and practices) and help the institution implement policies and practices to address these concerns. The use of external consultants may not necessarily be expensive if a network of institutions can be established, wherein a time/resource bank is created. In this way, individuals from several institutions work together as the external consultant group for one of the other institutions in the network; thus no money changes hands.

Extending Knowledge about Student Development

Student development theories are based on conventional assumptions compatible with logical positivism, not the emergent assumptions of indeterminism and chaos on which naturalistic research is based. A small number of individual case studies might be useful in understanding how students change over the course of college. Of course, individual case studies were the genesis of conventional student development theory (e.g., White, 1966). However, the purpose of using naturalistic methods is not to identify patterns of development that generalize to other students, but rather to identify commonalities and differences. Such information is sorely needed, particularly about students of color who have been underrepresented in previous studies and whose developmental processes may or may not be consistent with those described in student development theory and research (Stage, 1989). Also, the "chilly climate" often encountered by students of color and women may have a bearing on developmental processes. Without intensive case studies, it will not be possible to begin to ferret out and understand human development in an increasingly pluralistic academy.

A Note on Combining Quantitative and Qualitative Methods

". . . you should say what you mean," the March Hare went on.

"I do," Alice hastily replied; "at least—at least I mean what I say—that's the same thing you know."

"Not the same thing a bit!" said the Hatter. "Why, you might just as well say that 'I see what I eat' is the same thing as 'I eat what I see'!"

"You might just as well say," added the March Hare, "that 'I like what I get' is the same thing as 'I get what I like'!"

Alice's Adventures in Wonderland
Chapter VII: A Mad Tea-Party

Some have argued that the assumptions on which conventional and naturalistic research are based are not different points on a continuum, but rather are disjunct (Clark, 1985). A healthy debate has continued in the literature on this point (Smith & Heshusius, 1986). Some have argued that conventional and naturalistic methods cannot be used together. Others believe that for certain research questions, using conventional and naturalistic methods in concert is appropriate. Howe's (1988) paper on this topic is excellent. The issues are complicated and cannot be resolved here; rather, my purpose is to illustrate two obvious points. First, the integration of conventional and naturalistic data presents challenges (Jick, 1979). Second, conventional methods such as questionnaires, surveys, telephone checklist protocols and standardized instruments such as Pace's College Student Experience Questionnaire (CSEQ), even though they constrain the responses of participants, will continue to be used because they are relatively efficient ways of obtaining information from a large number of persons; also, the findings can be analyzed by computer.

What is a researcher to do if she or he wishes to combine conventional and naturalistic methods? The story of Janus is relevant. Janus, the mythical Roman god of portals and of beginnings and endings, is usually depicted as having two faces looking in opposite directions. Student affairs researchers will have to practice Janusian thinking by looking in front and behind at the same time and, with a little luck, find ways of integrating conventional and naturalistic data. Two examples are presented below.

In a study of institutional factors related to high quality out-of-class experiences of undergraduate students, the primary data collection methods were naturalistic, using the definition offered earlier (Kuh et al., 1991); about 1,300 people, including more than 600 students, at 14 colleges and universities were interviewed. Also, the CSEQ was administered. The CSEQ enabled us to learn more about patterns of involvement and the self-reported impact of involvement on personal development from approximately 3,600 students, thus increasing by sixfold the number of students participating in the study. The CSEQ data also permitted us to corroborate the perceptions of 48 experts who nominated the institutions to be included in the study.

Another example of combining conventional and qualitative methods is Chickering's evaluations of curricular experimentation at Goddard College. As Chickering (Thomas & Chickering, 1984) explained:

> I collected massive data through a comprehensive testing program involving 16 hours of achievement tests, personality inventories, and other instruments . . . These test results

were supplemented by diary information, which I collected from samples of students on a continuing basis and from more detailed interviews. . . My problem was to make sense of all this data I was gathering and to develop some conceptual framework . . . (pp. 392-93).

The conceptual framework that emerged is now known as the seven developmental vectors which served as the organizing framework for *Education and Identity* (Chickering, 1969).

Conventional and naturalistic data generate different pictures of the student experience. Each has advantages and disadvantages. Naturalistic methodologies require inquiry skills with which few researchers have training and experience. Most researchers are not trained in inductive analysis, such as creating specific units of data and moving from units of data to more general themes. Furthermore, naturalistic inquiry is labor intensive and thus expensive compared with conventional approaches. For example, written summaries of case reports should always be circulated for comments of participants, a process from which a great deal can be learned (Crowson, 1986); however, this is also very time consuming. Also, maintaining participants' confidentiality or anonymity, establishing trusting relationships in short periods of time, and the pressure for completely open negotiations that honor participants' interpretations are other issues that must be considered when using naturalistic methods.

Thus, there are trade-offs between the conventional and naturalistic approaches. The critical decision is whether the proposed methods will generate the range and depth of insights needed to understand the phenomenon being studied and to enable student affairs professionals and others to take appropriate action.

Conclusion

Alice tried a little to fancy to herself what such an extraordinary way of living would be like, but it puzzled her too much . . .

Alice's Adventures in Wonderland
Chapter VII: A Mad Tea-Party

During most of her wanderings through Wonderland, Alice was confused and disoriented. Student affairs researchers who learned to do conventional research grounded in logical positivism will find naturalistic methods puzzling; some will be skeptical that interviews, for example, can produce reliable and credible information. Because the credibility of student affairs as a field of professional practice among some faculty members and academic administrators is often tenuous, some student life researchers may consider it too great a risk to use naturalistic methods, when appropriate, in the place of conventional approaches that enjoy wide acceptance. Fortunately, in all disciplines the silent revolution is having an impact; naturalistic methods are being used with increasing frequency.

Assuming that knowledge gatekeepers, such as journal editors and manuscript reviewers, are open to alternative forms of knowing and creating knowledge, more naturalistic studies will begin to appear in student affairs journals as student affairs researchers become more familiar and gain experience with these methods. As with most innovations, the initial efforts will have to be of extremely high quality to be judged as good as a study using conventional methods. It is likely that for a period of time, people who submit for publication studies using naturalistic methods will have their work more carefully scrutinized than those who employ conventional methods.

Student affairs researchers can learn much from the work of colleagues in allied professional associations, such as the Association for the Study of Higher Education and the American Educational Research Association, where naturalistic research is featured. Most important, we must acknowledge what we do not know about naturalistic methods and take the necessary steps to increase our understanding of this type of research. Students and the student affairs profession will be the beneficiaries of our efforts.

References

Attinasi, Jr., L.C. (1989). Getting in: Mexican Americans' perceptions of university attendance and the implications for freshman year persistence. *Journal of Higher Education, 60,* 247-77.

Bartunek, J. (1984). Changing interpretive schemes and organizational restructuring: The example of a religious order. *Administrative Science Quarterly, 27,* 355-72.

Campbell, D.T., and Stanley, J.C. (1963). *Experimental and quasiexperimental designs for research.* Chicago: Rand McNally.

Caple, R.B. (1985). Counseling and the self-organization paradigm. *Journal of Counseling and Development, 64,* 173-78.

Caple, R.B. (1987). The change process in developmental theory: A self-organization paradigm, part 1. *Journal of College Student Personnel, 28,* 4-11.

Capra, F. (1983). *The turning point: Science, society, and the rising culture.* New York: Basic Books

Chickering, A.W. (1969). *Education and identity.* San Francisco: Jossey-Bass Publisher, Inc.

Clark, B.R. (1970). *The distinctive college: Reed, Antioch, and Swarthmore.* Chicago: Aldine.

Clark, B.R. (1984). *The higher education system: Academic organization in cross-national perspective.* Berkeley: University of California Press.

Clark, D.L. (1985). Emerging paradigms in organizational theory and research. In Y.S. Lincoln (ed.), *Organizational theory and inquiry: The paradigm revolution* (pp. 43-78). Beverly Hills: Sage.

Cooperrider, D.L., and Srivastva, S. (1987). Appreciative

inquiry in organizational life. *Research in Organizational Change and Development,* 1, 129-69.

Cronbach, L.J. (1975). Beyond the two disciplines of scientific psychology. *The American Psychologist,* 30(2), 116-26.

Cronbach, L.J. (1982). Prudent aspirations for social inquiry. In W. Kruskal (ed.), *The social sciences: Their nature and uses* (pp. 61-81). Chicago: University of Chicago Press.

Cronbach, L.J., and Snow, R.E. (1977). *Aptitudes and instructional methods.* New York: Irvington.

Crowson, R.L. (1986). Qualitative research methods in higher education. In J. Smart (ed.), *Handbook on theory and research in higher education* (vol. III, pp 1-56). New York: Agathon.

Cziko, G.A. (1989). Unpredictability and indeterminism in human behavior: Arguments and implications for educational research. *Educational Researcher,* 18(3), 17-25.

Fetterman, D.M. (1988). Qualitative approaches to evaluating education. *Educational Researcher,* 17(1), 17-23.

Dobbert, M.L. (1984). *Ethnographic research: Theory and application for modern schools and societies.* New York: Praeger.

Fleming, J. (1984). *Blacks in college.* San Francisco: Jossey-Bass Publisher, Inc.

Geertz, C. (1973). *The interpretation of cultures.* New York: Basic Books

Geertz, C. (1980) Blurred genres: The refiguration of social thought. *American Scholar,* 49, 165-79.

Glaser, B., and Strauss, A. (1967). *The discovery of grounded theory: Strategies for qualitative research.* Chicago: Aldine.

Gleick, J. (1987). *Chaos: Making a new science.* New York: Viking.

Goetz, J.P., and LeCompt, M.D. (1984). *Ethnography and qualitative design in educational research.* Orlando, FL: Academic.

Howard, G.S. (1985). Can research in the human sciences become more relevant to practice? *Journal of Counseling and Development,* 63, 539-44.

Howe, K.R. (1988). Against the quantitative-qualitative incompatibility thesis or dogmas die hard. *Educational Researcher,* 17(1), 10-16.

Jick, T.D. (1979). Mixing qualitative and quantitative methods: Triangulation in action. *Administrative Science Quarterly,* 24, 602-11.

Keller, G. (1985). Trees without fruit: The problem with research about higher education. *Change,* 17(1), 7-10.

Keller, G. (1986). Free at last? Breaking the chains that bind education research. *The Review of Higher Education,* 10, 129-34.

Kuh, G.D. (ed.).(1983). *Understanding student affairs organizations.* New Directions for Student Services, no. 23. San Francisco: Jossey-Bass Publisher, Inc.

Kuh, G.D. (1989). Organizational concepts and influences. In U. Delworth and G. Hanson (eds.), *Student services: A handbook for the profession* (rev. ed.) (pp. 209-42). San Francisco: Jossey-Bass Publisher, Inc.

Kuh, G.D. (1990). The demographic juggernaut. In M.J. Barr and M.L. Upcraft (eds.), *New futures for student affairs* (pp. 71-97). San Francisco: Jossey-Bass Publisher, Inc.

Kuh, G.D.; Bean, J.P.; Bradley, R.K.; and Coomes, M.D. (1986). Contributions of student affairs journals to the college student research. *Journal of College Student Personnel,* 27, 292-304.

Kuh, G.D.; Schuh, J.S.; Whitt, E.J.; Andreas, R.; Lyons, J.; Strange, C.; Krehbiel, L.; and MacKay, K. (1991). *Involving colleges: Encouraging learning and personal development through out-of-class experiences.* San Francisco: Jossey-Bass Publisher, Inc.

Kuh, G.D.; Whitt, E.J.; and Shedd, J.D. (1987). *Student affairs work, 2001: A paradigmatic odyssey.* Alexandria, VA: American College Personnel Association.

Lather, P. (1986). Research as praxis. *Harvard Educational Review,* 56, 257-77.

Lincoln, Y.S. (1986). A future-oriented comment on the state of the profession. *The Review of Higher Education,* 10, 135-42.

Lincoln, Y.S., and Guba, E. (1985). *Naturalistic inquiry.* Beverly Hills: Sage.

Lorenz, E.N. (1963). Deterministic nonperiodic flow. *Journal of the Atmospheric Sciences,* 20, 130-41.

Lorenz, E.N. (1979, December). Predictability: Does the flap of a butterfly's wings in Brazil set off a tornado in Texas? Paper presented at the annual meeting of the American Association for the Advancement of Science, Washington, D.C.

Lucas, C. (1985). Out at the edge: Notes on a paradigm shift. *Journal of Counseling and Development,* 64, 165-72.

Maruyama, M. (1976). Toward cultural symbiosis. In E. Jantsch and C.H. Waddington (eds.), *Evolution and consciousness: Human systems in transition* (pp. 198-213). Reading, MA: Addison-Wesley.

Merton, R.K.; Fisk, M.; and Kendall, P.L. (1956). *The focused interview.* New York: Free Press.

Miles, M.B., and Huberman, A.M. (1984). *Qualitative data analysis: A sourcebook of new methods.* Beverly Hills, CA: Sage.

Phillips, D.C. (1980). What do the researcher and the practitioner have to offer each other? *Educational Researcher,* 9(11), 17-24.

Popper, K.R. (1979). *Objective knowledge: An evolutionary approach* (rev. ed.). Oxford: Clarendon.

Prigogine, I., and Stengers, I. (1984). *Order out of chaos.* New York: Bantam Books.

Reinharz, S. (1978). *On becoming a social scientist.* San Francisco: Jossey-Bass Publisher, Inc.

Sanford, N. (1962). Higher education as a field of study. In N. Sanford (ed.), *The American college* (pp. 31-73). New York: Wiley.

Schwartz, P., and Ogilvy, J. (1979). The emergent paradigm: Changing patterns of thought and belief. Menlo Park, CA: SRI International Analytical Report No. 7, Values and Lifestyles Program.

Skrtic, T.M. (1985). Doing naturalistic research into educational organizations. In Y.S. Lincoln (ed.), *Organizational theory and inquiry: The paradigm revolution* (pp. 185-220). Beverly Hills, CA: Sage.

Smith, J.K., and Heshusius, L. (1986). Closing down the conversation: The end of the quantitative-qualitative debate among educational inquirers. *Educational Researcher,* 15, 4-12.

Snow, R.E. (1977). Individual differences and institutional theory. *Educational Researcher,* 6(10), 11-15.

Stage, F.K. (1989). College outcomes and student development: Filling the gaps. *The Review of Higher Education,* 12, 293-304.

Stake, R.E. (1978). The case study method in social inquiry. *Educational Researcher,* 7(2), 5-8.

Steele, S. (1989, February). The recoloring of campus life: Student racism, academic pluralism, and the end of a dream. *Harper's,* 47-55.

Terrell, M.C., and Wright, D.J. (eds.) (1988). *From survival to success: Promoting minority student retention.* Washington, D.C.: National Association of Student Personnel Administrators.

Thomas, R., and Chickering, A.W. (1984). Education and identity revisited. *Journal of College Student Personnel,* 25, 392-99.

Tierney, W.G. (1989). *Curricular landscapes, democratic vistas: Transformative leadership in higher education.* New York: Praeger.

Tripp, D.H. (1983). Co-authorship and negotiation: The interview as act of creation. *Interchange,* 14(3), 32-45.

White, R.W. (1966). *Lives in progress* (2nd ed.). New York: Holt, Rinehart & Winston.

Yin, R.K. (1984). *Case study research: Design and methods.* Beverly Hills: Sage.

Chapter 5

The Call to Assessment: What Role for Student Affairs?

Gary Hanson

"Give your evidence," said the King, "and don't be nervous, or I'll have you executed on the spot."
Alice's Adventures in Wonderland
Chapter XI: Who Stole the Tarts?

Higher education can certainly sympathize with Alice. For the last ten years, the King (nearly everyone outside higher education) has been telling us that we have a problem. The problem is: Taxpayers are paying large sums of money to educate students and they believe too many of these students leave college without knowing how to read, compute, write, or think. Neither have these students developed leadership ability, social skills, or moral character. The accountability finger of our major funding sources—state legislators, boards of trustees, private donors, and corporate business and industry—is pointed directly at higher education. And much like Alice, we are nervous. The risks are high. What if higher education doesn't have the evidence? Evidence for what? We don't know what the King wants and that is why we are nervous.

Within the ivy-covered walls of academe, we are confident in our assumptions that students learn; we see evidence of it every day. Students who leave college with a degree are very different people than the ones who arrived at the gates to our college campuses four or five years earlier. So why is the King demanding evidence? Doesn't higher education spend great sums of money on the instructional budget; expand the number of books in the library each year; add the latest equipment to the research labs; and construct sparkling, clean, multimillion dollar classrooms, residence halls, and student centers? Haven't the average college admission test scores of our entering freshmen risen every year for the last five years? Can't the King see the quality of our educational efforts?

Ahh, yes! the King watches with great interest, but uses a different definition of quality. The King now defines the quality of higher education in terms of student outcomes. What have students learned at your institution? Can you show that your efforts have contributed to that learning? Quality is no longer defined in terms of the academic characteristics of the entering freshman class or the number of books in the library or the number of new buildings. A quality education is one in which the student learns—and you had better have the evidence.

The Wonderland of Assessment in Higher Education

In response to the demands for evidence, interest in assessing student growth and development has seen a remarkable resurgence in the last few years. Student affairs has long given lip service to assessment. Our early philosophical position statement, the *Student Personnel Point of View* (ACE, 1937), strongly recommended that we assess students. However, over the years interest waned and assessment of college students seemed less important. Our goals were difficult to measure and demanded a great deal of effort. Why worry about all those fuzzy concepts? How could we possibly assess critical thinking, communication skills, leadership, or ethical judgment?

Today, we must assess! We are being asked to show that what we do makes a difference in how and what students learn, both inside the classroom and out. How can student affairs professionals respond to the demands to "show us your evidence?" What roles can we play in demonstrating the quality of our educational products—learning and development? There are several. First, we must understand the issues that undergird the assessment movement and this redefinition of quality that has taken place. Second, before we can show that we are effective in facilitating learning, we must understand the problems inherent in assessing the effects of what we do. These methodological problems are not insignificant. Third, we must create new solutions. The King has little faith in our history. We must find new ways to ask important questions and we must diversify our attempts to find the answers. Finally, we must span the boundaries of our ordinary work setting and assume new roles on campus. We must lead in conceptualizing, planning, coordinating, conducting, and disseminating our assessment efforts. Most important, we must become disciples of assessment and believe that assessment will help establish the validity and integrity of what we do.

Assessment Issues in Higher Education

Why has assessment become such a focal issue in higher education today? The quality of what we do has been questioned and assessment is seen as a response, a way to answer our critics. By examining the way we educate/develop students (process), we assess how they learn. By measuring the outcomes of the college experience (product), we assess what students learn. To effectively use assessment, student affairs professionals must understand this distinction and the related issues that underlie the assessment agenda. At first glance, the two major goals of assessment (improvement and accountability) seem to be in conflict.

How can we use assessment data to show that we are accountable and to improve our daily practice? With care and planning, assessment data can be used to serve multiple purposes: to diagnose and describe, to monitor student behavior, and to evaluate and make judgments.

Conflict of Goals

As noted, there is at first glance apparent conflict between the two major goals of assessment. Essentially, the problem is how to use assessment data for dual purposes: to improve the educational process and to account for what is learned. To improve the quality of education requires that we collect data that explains how students learn. Faculty and staff in and outside the classroom need information about conditions of learning, types of learners, and what kinds of processes facilitate student growth and learning. Hutchings (1989) called this "looking behind student outcomes" to focus on how and why students learn and suggested the following questions be raised to better understand the process behind student outcomes:

What do we know about students who enter our institution?
How are course-taking patterns related to outcomes?
How do students experience the institution?
What is the student's contribution to learning?
What do students learn over time in a program of study?
How do out-of-class experiences contribute to learning?
What are students able to do with what they know?
What patterns characterize students' movement through the institution?
What judgments can students make about their learning? (p. 1)

By searching for the answers to these questions, an institution can begin to make the connection between desired outcomes and what must be done to make them happen. Improvement requires attention to the final results, but more importantly the assessment process must yield information about the context and process that either facilitated or hindered the attainment of important educational outcomes.

To be accountable to the external public, higher education has been asked to document what students learn. A growing number of states have mandated student outcomes assessment (National Governors' Association, 1988). Obtaining a degree from college is no longer sufficient evidence that students have learned or that what they learned is important. Evidence that students can read, write, compute, think, and communicate now forms the basis for much of the student outcomes movement. In addition, more and more states are suggesting that the noncognitive components of learning are equally important, and they too must be documented. New Jersey, for example, has legislated that student development outcomes will be assessed; that colleges provide evidence of growth and learning in student involvement, satisfaction, and personal development (COEP, 1987).

Ewell (1987) has discussed this conflict of emphasis on what students learn and how students learn in terms of assessment for accountability (what) and assessment for improvement (how). Though seemingly in conflict, these goals are actually interrelated. As we learn more about the educational process of how students learn, the quality of the students leaving college should improve and our accountability to the external public should increase. It is only in the short term that the relationship between these goals creates a problem. The issue really becomes: What resources will it take to pursue both goals? Not only are the questions different, but the assessment strategies to pursue the answers are necessarily different as well. Can we legitimately commit to pursuing both goals? Are the time, staff, and money available? A related concern is where to start. If the focus on the assessment effort is on the improvement of practice, it may take too long to find the answers and an impatient public will withdraw the support that it takes to become more accountable. On the other hand, if time and effort are spent primarily on establishing what students learn, the results may only show what the external public already assumes to be true—that students have not learned enough. Unfortunately, the focus on outcomes leaves the institution with insufficient information about how to change or how to improve student development. Therein lies the short-term conflict between the assessment goals of improvement and accountability. The challenge to colleges and universities is to find ways to provide information on outcomes to meet the public's demands, while concurrently turning its attention to understanding and improving the structures, events, and processes that affect student outcomes.

The Multiple Purposes of Assessment

Effective utilization of assessment data demands an understanding of the purposes of assessment. Different purposes require different types of data, data collection strategies, data analysis techniques, and reporting formats. Analyzing the purpose to be accomplished for a particular assessment project aids in structuring what is to be done, when it should be done, how it should be done, and who should be involved.

The reasons for conducting an assessment can be subsumed under three general purposes:

- Diagnosis
- Monitoring
- Evaluation

Understanding how the assessment process differs when each of these purposes drives the assessment project will aid the design of more effective assessment strategies.

Diagnosis. The purpose behind diagnosis is to understand more about the current status of students, programs, or institutions. Diagnosis typically aids in identifying problems, but diagnostic assessment information may also highlight positive aspects or characteristics of people, programs, and institutions as well. Assessment data collected for diagnosis is primarily descriptive in nature and the collection of assessment data for this purpose usually occurs at one point in time. The results describe the characteristics or status of something in a given context at a specific point in time. For example, students may be assessed during orientation to diagnose their level of academic preparation in English, mathematics, foreign language, or other academic subjects. Data may also be collected from students as they exit the college or university to determine their reasons for leaving. The results provide diagnostic information about student and institutional problems and/or successes. Collecting information about the need for, utilization of, and satisfaction with student service programs is another example of diagnostic information. High demand for a service coupled with low utilization or low satisfaction provides information to a program director for initiating changes in the delivery of the service. The questions that undergird this assessment purpose focus on: What is the current state of affairs? Is there a problem? Examples of diagnostic assessment by student affairs professionals include placement testing, learning skills assessment for remediation (or in the case of many learning disabilities, compensation), career assessment for academic advising and career counseling, and program needs assessment.

Monitoring. Assessment data can also be used to monitor how and when the characteristics of students, programs, and institutions change or vary over time. To effectively use data for monitoring change, data must be collected across several points in time. Data collected for diagnosis may form the foundation for monitoring students, programs, and institutions across time, but the data must be collected repeatedly (systematically) and it must be collected from representative samples within the population of interest at each data collection point. This type of data utilization vastly improves the information system needed by administrators making educational policy decisions. For example, by monitoring trends in student characteristics, student affairs professionals can help to address such questions as: Is the academic preparation of students today better or worse than it was five years ago? How have students' attitudes toward religion changed from the time when their parents were in school? Are students as satisfied with their housing as students five years ago?

In addition to monitoring the characteristics of groups of students, assessment data can also be used to monitor individual student progress. A student's academic transcript is a good example of an unobtrusive measure that is used in monitoring individual student progress. The sequence of courses and the student's grade performance are maintained from semester to semester and from year to year. This kind of data allows the student and the college to assess the level of progress toward meeting the institution's requirements for graduation. Monitoring individual student progress outside the classroom also has merit. For example, Brown and Citrin (1977) suggested that student involvement in campus learning experiences outside the classroom could be monitored using a "developmental transcript." This type of information gives the student and the college the ability to review the kinds of educational programs students experience. Monitoring these kinds of data can lead to productive changes in the cocurricular opportunities available on a given campus.

Another important "monitoring" use of assessment data is to track students' participation in specific programs. For example, student participation in a college's recruitment or retention programs can be monitored. Over a period of time, the success of these programs to attract or retain students can be compared with previous history or with the impact of other programs. The emphasis of this use is less on individual student progress as it is on changes in the program over time. Research questions might include some of the following: Do the recruitment programs attract the same number and types of students as they did five years ago? Has the nature of enrolled students changed in any way? Do students who participate in certain retention programs graduate at a higher rate or in a shorter period of time than similar students who do not participate? Without monitoring such data, it is difficult to know when a program is successful or in need of an overhaul.

Assessment data can also be used to monitor global changes in the institution. For example, colleges may be interested in monitoring the number of students who find jobs in careers related to their college major, or they may want to know how many students continue their education in graduate school. Or, they may want to monitor changes in the ratio of faculty to students, or the ratio of student affairs professionals to students, or the amount of money budgeted for student development programs relative to the amount of money budgeted for classroom instructional purposes. Information of this type is an indicator of institutional health or vitality.

Evaluation. Perhaps the most complex use of assessment data is to make summative judgments about students, programs, or the institution. Data used for evaluation focus on the merit or worth of a particular effort. Deciding the worth of a particular effort requires that the "costs" of the effort be weighed against the "benefits" derived from the effort. The costs weighed can be tangible, such as time or money, or they can be intangible, including such things as psychological stress, emotional effect, or lost opportunities. The benefits, likewise, can be both tangible and intangible. As examples of benefit indicators, students may earn degrees, be employed, or be elected class president. They may also gain self-confidence, increase their appreciation of people from different backgrounds, or leave campus with a greater desire to help other, less fortunate individuals. Student affairs professionals may weigh the costs of working weekends and evenings against the benefits of the satisfaction derived from fostering leadership within a student organization. A college president might want to weigh the costs of buying books for the library or raising a salary offer to attract a counseling center director against the benefits that would accrue to the institution.

When making judgments about a program it is useful to make a distinction about the purpose of the evaluation. Data can be used to evaluate the overall utility or worth of a program, typically called a summative evaluation, or data can be used to evaluate the process of the program, usually called a formative evaluation. Different questions are asked, depending upon whether the primary interest is formative or summative. Some evaluations may require doing both.

When the interest is on evaluating process, data must be collected to illustrate how the effort came about. How much time did it take? When did it start? When did it finish? What happened along the way? What are the conditions that contributed to any observed change? The judgment of worth is made in terms of the efficiency of the process, on the qualitative nature of what transpired, and on the re-sources required to accomplish the particular effort. The major decision that must be made is whether changing the process will increase the likelihood that a particular goal can be reached in a timely fashion. Is changing the process worth the cost given the particular benefits that may accrue?

When the focus of evaluation data is on outcomes, data are used to answer these types of questions: Was the desired goal achieved? Did the effort change the status of the indi-viduals or programs or institutions involved? Did the stu-dent, program, or institution achieve other unanticipated goals? Each of these questions focuses on the outcome or product of some effort, and a summative judgment of worth must be made relative to the costs of achieving the outcome. If only half of the students who complete a comprehensive retention program effort graduate, is that enough of a ben-efit to continue the effort? What should be done if the pro-gram only seems to help white, middle-class men? Can the college continue to spend $1,000 or $2,000 or $5,000 to re-cruit a single student?

Student affairs professionals will be involved in using assessment data for each of these varied purposes: diagnosing, monitoring, and evaluating. Perhaps the most important item to remember is that before assessment begins, one must thoroughly understand the purpose behind it. Knowing the purpose of assessment will help focus the questions and lead to better use of the assessment results.

Methodological Assessment Issues

While the assessment of student development outcomes may occur near the end point of students' college experiences, there is an underlying interest in the process that led to that development; that is, how did students grow, develop or learn? What contributed to the learning? If the reason for doing the outcomes assessment is for accountability reasons, one would want to know: Did our programs make a difference?

Once these questions are asked, a wide range of methodological issues are introduced into the assessment of student development outcomes. This section describes methodological problems with the assessment of student development that must be settled prior to measurement. The interested reader may want to consult the following articles for a more detailed discussion of these methodological issues: Baird (1988), Ewell (1987, 1988), and Hanson (1982, 1988).

The methodological issues that require the most attention in assessing student development are: (a) selecting the dimension(s) of student development, (b) using appropriate assessment methods, and (c) choosing developmental timeframes.

Selecting the Dimension(s) of Student Development

Selecting which dimensions to measure is a necessary first step in selecting appropriate instruments. In an early review of student development outcomes taxonomies, Lenning

(1977) found literally hundreds of ways to conceptualize the ways students grow and develop. Some taxonomies he reviewed focused exclusively on cognitive development while others focused on psychosocial development. A common theme was that multiple dimensions were found across all the taxonomies. However, there is little agreement across taxonomies and, within any given taxonomy, important dimensions may have been omitted. When measuring student development outcomes, one must be aware that most assessment instruments measure only a limited number of dimensions. Even those instruments closely tied to a theoretical perspective, for example the Student Development Task Inventory (SDTI), may only measure a restricted number of dimensions. For this reason, measuring the full range of student development outcomes may require the administration of several instruments. An example of the latter problem is the set of instruments developed by Hood (1986) and others to measure Chickering's (1969) vectors of student development. Assessing a full range of student development outcomes may require a considerable expenditure of time, effort, and money.

Using Appropriate Assessment Methods

There is a rich variety of methods and techniques for assessing student development outcomes. The problem with using any one method is that the developmental process may vary across dimensions, and a scoring technique that is appropriate for one dimension may not be appropriate for a different dimension. Different methods produce different results. Rest (1976) defined three frequently used methods: preference, comprehension, and spontaneous use (production). According to Mines (1982), various measurement formats have been used to assess preferences (Likert-type scales), comprehension (asking students to paraphrase or match statements), or production (open-ended or structured interviews). The production format is useful in basic developmental research because the responses provide a rich database for refining theory and understanding the developmental process. One problem with this method is that it is very time consuming and expensive. The preference or comprehension methods typically use Likert scales or multiple choice items to identify or classify the level or stage of development. These methods are more likely to be used when assessing student development outcomes.

Another methodological issue related to the different assessment techniques is that different scoring methods produce different results (Rest, 1976). Scoring methods range from using the highest scored stage, to the percentage of highest stage exhibited, to the modal level of stage used, to the use of cutting scores based on cumulative distributions of stage typical responses. For a more thorough discussion of these issues, see Mines (1982).

Choosing Developmental Timeframes

When designing a student development outcomes assessment, one of the first decisions that must be made is whether the status of the outcome (the end product) is the only variable of interest or whether there is an interest in assessing how that change came about. The difference in emphasis can best be summarized by asking which of these two questions needs to be answered:

1. What is the highest level or stage of development that has been attained?

2. Is the student at a higher stage of development at this point in time than at an earlier point in time?

The first question can be answered by assessing the student at one point in time, but the second question involves assessing change over time. Different strategies of assessment are needed, different instruments may be needed, and different statistical treatment of the data are needed. Deciding which of these two questions (or both) needs an answer will depend on the purposes of the assessment discussed previously in this chapter. When there is an interest in assessing the degree or amount of change, additional methodological issues become important.

Numerous authors have written about the problems with assessing change over time (Bereiter, 1963; Cronbach & Furby, 1970; Hanson, 1982, 1988; Harris, 1963; Linn, 1981; and Pascarella, 1987). There are two categories of problems. One problem is that most assessment instruments were designed to measure status at a single point in time, and are not sensitive to measuring change in a construct over time. The second problem is that change in any given developmental dimension is negatively correlated with the level of the student's initial status. (This relationship is a statistical artifact of the measurement error of the assessment instrument.) Stated another way, the lower a student is at the first assessment, the greater the change possible when measured at a later time. If students are at a high level at the time of the first measurement, the only direction they are likely to change is to a lower level, if they change at all. A more complete discussion of these problems is available in Baird (1988) and Hanson (1988).

New Questions, New Solutions

Prior to 1980, our working assumptions about student development derived from the work of Erikson (1968), Kohlberg (1964), Perry (1970), and Chickering (1969). Most of these theories assumed that human development occurred in a sequential, orderly, and cumulative process. However, these assumptions have been questioned (Allen, 1989; Baruch, Barnett & Rivers, 1983; Belenky, Clinchy, Goldberger & Tarule, 1986; Gilligan, 1982; Josselson, 1987). As Allen (1989) pointed out, human development may be much more individualistic, fluid, nonlinear, multi-optioned, and interconnected. In addition to changes in the assumptions about human development, there is growing evidence that individually experienced events, culture, environment, context, and setting have considerable influence on how and when students develop. Most current assessment instruments are based on our old assumptions that development is linear, sequential, cumulative, and orderly (Hanson, 1982; Mines, 1982). There is a gap, a large gap, between our current thinking about student development and the assessment instruments we use to document that student development occurs.

New Questions

Given the gap between new assumptions about student development and the unavailability of newer assessment instruments, new questions and assessment strategies are needed. Allen (1989) raised the following as new directions for our research questions:

1. Are there single or multiple pathways of development?

2. What is the "shape" of development? Does development follow prescribed stages or do individual patterns of development occur that are highly influenced by culture, background, context, and motivations?

3. What triggers development in an individual? Is development age related or is development triggered by external and internal conditions?

4. Do different patterns of development occur within different generational cohorts? Does the nature of development change depending on the particular generational cohort being studied? Will future generations of college students develop in different ways than those in the past?

5. Can human development be assessed in a fragmented manner? Or can development only be assessed holistically?

All these questions take issue with our traditional assumptions about human development. With the questioning of the assumptions comes the need to re-examine our assessment strategies. Most of the studies that have questioned our traditional developmental assumptions have used qualitative research methodology and have operated from the naturalistic, rather than the positivistic paradigm of inquiry (see Chapter Four for a more detailed discussion of these two paradigms). If we are to pursue new questions, old assessment strategies should be discarded and replaced with assessment techniques that broaden the kinds of data we collect.

New Strategies

How does one go about assessing student developmental outcomes? The choice of which method(s) to use must be based on a combination of cost, administration time, staff expertise, interpretability of the results, sophistication of the end user audience, and, of course, the use that will be made of the data. A brief explanation of several assessment strategies will aid in the selection of a technique most appropriate for a given campus assessment project. Lenning (1988) identified six traditional assessment methods or strategies frequently used to assess noncognitive educational outcomes:

- observable performance measures
- self-report measures
- consensus-rendering techniques
- inventories
- simulations
- secondary data applications.

Each strategy may be useful for a given student population and purpose of assessment. However, as Lenning (1988) pointed out, "Every measure has weaknesses; where one is weak, another may be strong. Multiple measures improve overall reliability and validity, without the excessive costs of designing a single instrument that would have the required degree of stability" (p. 49).

Observable performance measures. These have long been used by faculty in the classroom to assess student performance. Work samples, oral presentations, team projects, debates, or group problem-solving experiences, in-basket tasks, and leaderless group discussions are just a few of the many techniques used. These techniques also work well in assessing student developmental outcomes such as team work, leadership, or the ability to understand others' point of view. One commercial example of an assessment technique using this approach is the ACT COMP, a work sample instrument widely used to assess important student outcomes.

Self-reports. These are among the most widely used assessment techniques in higher education and they provide a convenient method for collecting data about student developmental outcomes. Students may use this technique to report their perceptions of an educational experience as well as the impact of that experience on their lives. Self-report techniques also provide an easy way for students to report their level of involvement in campus activities or the level of achievement or accomplishment of important educational goals.

There are many ways to collect self-report information. The two most common methods are paper-and-pencil questionnaires and the interview. Both techniques can be used with an individual or with groups of students. Two less frequently used techniques, but ones that yield important data, are the Critical Incident Technique and the Behavioral Events Interview. The former technique allows students to identify important areas of growth or learning and provides an opportunity to report the critical factors that either facilitated or hindered their growth. The Behavioral Events Interview is used to identify the behavioral events that students believe to have caused specific positive or negative outcomes. The interviews typically take two or more hours but provide a rich database of anecdotal evidence about student development outcomes.

Consensus-rendering techniques. These constitute an important assessment technique because they allow diverse participants in the assessment process (such as students, faculty, administrators, and outside experts) to debate, discuss, and eventually reach agreement regarding whether an outcome has been achieved, and how it came about. Some examples of these consensus-rendering techniques include debates, juries, hearings, staffing conferences, as well as the focused Delphi technique, campus intelligence systems, and the use of the charette technique. The latter two techniques are more commonly used outside higher education, but offer interesting variations to more traditional assessment techniques. The "intelligence system" is labor intensive because it requires a network of individuals working together to compare information they know about a specific topic. The technique has been most widely used in police and military settings and by weather forecasting experts.

Inventories. Next to self-report measures, inventories are frequently used to assess student development outcomes. This category of assessment typically uses either multiple or single item scales to assess student development characteristics. Often inventories are standardized and commercially distributed, but many good inventories are also developed for local campus use as well. One advantage of using standardized inventories is the availability of normative information. Norms allow a comparison of the student from a local campus with students from other similar institutions. Caution must be used to make sure the two groups of students are comparable. Comparing traditional-age students with students older than average or using an instrument with normative information developed on only male students with female students would be inappropriate. A wide range of available instruments are reviewed in the *Ninth Mental Measurements Yearbook* (Mitchell, 1985). The interested reader should consult this publication for a thorough critique before selecting any assessment instrument for use.

Simulations. This category includes a diverse array of techniques ranging from role playing to case studies to interactive computer programs to in-basket analysis techniques. All simulations require the active participation of the student and are used for classroom instruction as often as they are for the assessment of outcomes. The assessment of decision making, oral communication and public speaking, and modes of cognitive thinking style are examples of student development outcomes that could be assessed using the simulation technique. The disadvantage of this technique is that it is time consuming and restricted to relatively small numbers of students unless some form of interactive computer software has been developed.

Secondary data applications. Before beginning any assessment project, it is worth the time and effort to search the campus for existing evidence of student data that may be used to supplement, clarify, and understand the primary assessment data from a more formal project. Grades, test scores, and results from earlier campus surveys help to define the nature of the campus student population. This information may facilitate the selection of students for a subsequent assessment project or it may be used as a baseline for interpreting the results of a small, more selective sample of students representing a particular field of study, residence hall, or age level.

All these assessment strategies may aid in the pursuit of information that better explains how, when, and to what degree students learn in the college setting. When the goal is improvement, many of these techniques will yield rich information about the process of student development. Using these techniques will give us a better understanding of the conditions of learning for many distinct populations of students. These techniques may not be as useful for establishing accountability of what we do. At first, there may be some reluctance to use some of the qualitative methods to document that students learn. However, as we gain greater experience with these techniques, we will improve our ability to report them in useful ways and to make them meaningful to our external public.

New Roles for Student Affairs Professionals

The increased emphasis on assessment in higher education has created a great opportunity for student affairs professionals to assume a pivotal role on campus today. We not only have a history of interest in assessment issues, but we have initiated new questions and assessment strategies to document what we know about student growth and development. In addition, we are beginning to understand what factors facilitate that learning and to what extent our programs and services have contributed to it. With this experience and knowledge base, student affairs professionals can assume the following kinds of roles in the assessment:

Conceptualizer. Every assessment project needs an idea person. The conceptualizer stimulates discussion among campus assessment committee members about the questions that need to be asked. Questions may include: What do we mean by learning or by development? What are our working assumptions about how development occurs on this campus? Who are the facilitators of learning and development on campus? The list could go on, but these questions illustrate how the conceptualizer can be involved in the initial stages of an assessment project. The satisfaction from assuming this role comes from the opportunity to broaden the definition of student learning and development beyond the confines of the classroom experience. If student affairs professionals ignore this important role, both students and the campus as a whole suffer from a diminished definition of learning and development.

Planner. Before assessment begins, a multitude of plans must be made. For useful assessment to occur, planning the assessment process should take as much time as conducting the assessment. Careful thought must be given to many different aspects of the total assessment project. Who or what should be assessed? When is the best time to conduct the assessment? How will implications about the development process influence how many times students are assessed? What instruments will measure the dimensions of student growth and learning that are important to this campus? Do those instruments need to be pilot tested? Are the procedures for data collection and analysis going to yield data that will answer our questions? What kind of data will our consumer audience understand? How much will the assessment cost? What are the limitations of this assessment plan? Are there better ways to conduct this assessment? Are there better ways to answer this particular set of questions? Are there political, social, or cultural reasons for not conducting the assessment? Is the campus community ready for the answers? How can we best deal with negative evidence? All these questions and many more become an issue for the student affairs professional involved in the day-to-day planning of a campus-wide assessment project. Detailed, day-to-day work schedules must be made in advance of any assessment project. The ultimate success of any assessment effort depends to a great extent on the ability of the planner to anticipate the unexpected problems.

Coordinator. Once the assessment project is planned and a blueprint or set of guidelines is developed for conducting the assessment, the work of implementing the assessment project begins. Student affairs professionals familiar with assessment procedures are needed to ensure that the conditions of assessment will facilitate the collection of useful information. An appropriate climate for assessment must be established on campus so students recognize the importance of participating. Materials must be ordered, students contacted, and completed materials scored and prepared for computer analysis. In addition to the project management details, another important aspect of the coordinator's responsibility is to communicate the progress of the assessment project to other campus assessment committee members and to other individuals with a vested interest in the outcome. The assessment of student outcomes has campus-wide implications and everyone will be interested in the results of the project. The coordinator has the responsibility of keeping interest in the project visible, but at the same time maintaining the quality and integrity of the data collection effort.

Research Technician. The role of research technician is that of quality assurance. Effective assessment requires that once the data are collected, it is accurately coded, summarized, scored (if necessary), and maintained in an easily accessible manner. When large numbers of students are included in an assessment project, the technician may need to use computerized records to archive the assessment data for each student. This role is particularly crucial when longitudinal research designs covering multiple years are needed to show developmental change. Maintaining records for qualitative assessment designs is equally important because the volume of information is enormous and the synthesis and analysis of the data is more complex. The technician for an assessment project is also responsible for advising the planners and coordinators of assessment about the most appropriate designs for a given assessment goal. Working knowledge of a wide variety of assessment strategies, research designs, modes of inquiry, and computer systems is necessary for the research technician.

Interpreter. Perhaps the most important role in the assessment process is that of interpreter. Making sense of the data requires skills in a variety of data analysis techniques, but more important, it requires a thorough understanding of how the college campus works. What kind of data do the key decision makers want? Do they prefer verbal reports to extensive tables of numbers? Do the consumers of the assessment results understand the strengths and weaknesses of quantitative and qualitative data reports? How can we communicate negative evidence and facilitate the change that may be needed within a particular department? To do the job of interpretation well, the interpreter must understand the political atmosphere on campus. What are the risks and rewards of disseminating the data too early—or worse, communicating the results too late? Can the sources of resistance to assessment be identified? Can they be included in the assessment process? Most important, the interpreter must recognize how data can be communicated to support the goals of improvement and accountability.

Summary

While it may sound as though these many different roles are relatively independent of one another, in fact, they are highly interrelated. While one individual need not assume all roles, it is crucial that the roles be coordinated. The interpreter of the data should be involved with the conceptualizer and planner to collect data that will be timely, understandable, and communicable. Likewise, the technician must alert the coordinator and planner and conceptualizer to key design features that may require additional students, different techniques and strategies for the collection of the data, and possible problems with the analysis of certain kinds of data. All these roles provide student affairs professionals an opportunity to be involved and to contribute to a better understanding of how students learn and the role our programs play in that learning.

References

Allen, K.E. (1989, June). A Non-linear model of student development: Implications for Assessment. Paper presented at American Association for Higher Education Assessment Forum, Atlanta, Georgia.

American Council on Education (1937). *Student personnel point of view.* American Council on Education Studies, Series 1, volume 1, number 3. Washington, DC: American Council on Education.

Baird, L.L. (1988). Value added: Using student gains as yardsticks of learning. In C. Adelman (ed.), *Performance and judgment* (pp. 205-16). Washington, DC: U.S. Department of Education, Office of Educational Research and Improvement.

Baruch, G.; Barnett, R.; and Rivers, C. (1983). *Life prints: New patterns of love and work for today's women.* New York: New American Library.

Belenky, M.F.; Clinchy, B.M.; Goldberger, N.R.; and Tarule, J.M. (1986). *Women's ways of knowing.* New York: Basic Books.

Bereiter, C. (1963). Some persisting dilemmas in the measurement of change. In C.W. Harris (ed.), *Problems in the measurement of change.* Madison, WI: University of Wisconsin Press.

Brown, R.D., and Citrin, R.S. (1977). A student development transcript: Assumptions, uses, and formats. *Journal of College Student Personnel,* 18(3), 163-68.

Chickering, A. (1969). *Education and identity.* San Francisco: Jossey-Bass Publisher, Inc.

Cronbach, L.J., and Furby, L. (1970). How we should measure change—or should we? *Psychological Bulletin,* 74, 68-80.

College Outcomes Evaluation Program (COEP). (1987). Report to the New Jersey Board of Higher Education from the Advisory Committee of the College Outcomes Evaluation Program. Trenton, NJ: Board of Higher Education for the State of New Jersey.

Erikson, E.H. (1968). *Identity, youth, and crisis.* New York: W.W. Norton.

Ewell, P.T. (1987). *Assessment, accountability and improvement: Managing the contradiction.* Boulder, CO: National Center for Higher Education Management Systems.

Ewell, P.T. (1988). *Implementing assessment: Some organizational issues.* In T.W. Banta (ed.), Implementing outcomes assessment: Promise and perils. New Directions for Institutional Research, No. 59. San Francisco: Jossey-Bass Publisher, Inc.

Gilligan, C. (1982). *In a different voice: Psychological theory and women's development.* Cambridge, MA: Harvard University Press.

Hanson, G.R. (1982). Critical issues in the assessment of student development. In G.R. Hanson (ed.), *Measuring student development.* New Directions for Student Services, No. 20. San Francisco: Jossey-Bass Publisher, Inc.

Hanson, G.R. (1988). Critical issues in the assessment of value added in education. In T.W. Banta (ed.), *Implementing outcomes assessment: Promise and perils.* (pp. 53-67). New Directions for Institutional Research, No. 59. San Francisco: Jossey-Bass Publisher, Inc.

Harris, C. (1963). *Problems in the measurement of change.* Madison, WI: University of Wisconsin Press.

Hood, A.B. (1986). *The Iowa student development inventories.* Iowa City, IA: HiTech Press.

Hutchings, P. (1989). Behind outcomes: Contexts and questions for assessment. A resource paper from the AAHE Assessment Forum. Washington, DC: American Association for Higher Education.

Josselson, R. (1987). *Finding herself: Pathways to identity development in women.* San Francisco: Jossey-Bass Publisher, Inc.

Kohlberg, L. (1964). Development of moral character and moral ideology. In M.L. Hoffman and L.W. Hoffman (ed.)., *Review of child development research.* Volume 1. New York: Russel Sage Foundation.

Lenning, O.T. (1977). *Previous attempts to structure educational outcomes and outcome-related concepts: A compilation and review of the literature.* Boulder, CO: National Center for Higher Education Management Systems.

Lenning, O.T. (1988). Use of noncognitive measures in assessment. In T.W. Banta (ed.), *Implementing outcomes assessment: Promise and perils.* New Directions for Institutional Research, No. 59. San Francisco: Jossey-Bass Publisher, Inc.

Linn, R.L. (1981). Measuring pretest-posttest performance changes. In R. Berk (ed.), *Educational evaluation methodology: The state of the art* (pp. 84-109), Baltimore: Johns Hopkins University Press.

Mines, R.A. (1982). Student development assessment techniques. In G.R. Hanson (ed.), *Measuring student development.* New Directions for Student Services, No. 20. San Francisco: Jossey-Bass Publisher, Inc.

Mitchell, Jr., J.R. (1985). *The ninth mental measurements yearbook* (2 vols.). Lincoln: University of Nebraska Press.

National Governors' Association (1988, January 5). *Developing state policy on college student assessment. Capital Ideas.* Washington, DC: National Governors' Association.

Pascarella, E.T. (1987). Some methodological and analytic issues in assessing the influence of college. Paper presented at a joint meeting of the American College Personnel Association and the National Association of Student Personnel Administrators, Chicago.

Perry, W.C. (1970). *Intellectual and ethical development in the college years.* New York: Holt, Rinehart and Winston.

Rest, J.R. (1976). *Development in judging moral issues.* Minneapolis: University of Minnesota Press.

Chapter 6

Peering Through the "Looking Glass" at Preparation Needed for Student Affairs Research

Deborah Ellen Hunter
Karl J. Beeler

"Have some wine?" the March Hare said in an encouraging tone.

Alice looked all round the table, but there was nothing on it but tea. "I don't see any wine," she remarked.

"There isn't any," said the March Hare.

"Then it wasn't very civil of you to offer it," said Alice angrily.

Alice's Adventures in Wonderland
Chapter VII: A Mad Tea-Party

Empty offers are uncivil. If student affairs professionals are to fulfill the promise offered by research, then they must develop the competencies and enthusiasms needed for its practice. Currently most master's degree programs (CAS, 1986) and all doctoral programs (Kuh, Lardy & Greenlee, 1979) in higher education and student affairs expect graduates to have acquired at least a modest level of skill in inquiry activities. Yet the acquisition of merely a minimal level of research competence fails to sustain interest in inquiry activities beyond graduate school, for the proportion of student affairs professionals conducting research subsequent to their graduate work is very, very small (Hunter & Kuh, 1987).

Most student affairs workers are service-oriented practitioners with a love-hate relationship with research: research is acknowledged as being necessary to advance the status of the profession and to contribute to professional practice, yet is an activity for which members display little enthusiasm and to which they give low priority among their professional responsibilities. In shaping professional roles and the place within the academy for student affairs, few within the profession have accepted the challenge of developing a "research mentality" (Brown, 1972, p. 41). Nonetheless, it has become increasingly critical to broaden the participation of student affairs professionals in shaping research questions, pursuing study of pressing issues on the campus, and contributing to the profession's knowledge base. Only then can all members of the profession fulfill the expectation set forth in *A Perspective on Student Affairs:* to function as "experts on students and their environments" (NASPA, 1987, p. 14).

This chapter explores the roles both graduate preparation programs and professional associations can play in fostering the research orientations of all members of higher education and student affairs profession.

For new members of the profession, graduate school provides the most likely setting for acquiring the skills and sparking the curiosities important for inquiry activities. If today's graduate students do not "catch the spirit" for engaging in inquiry activities and are not taught how to conduct research on issues of relevance to professional practice, how can student affairs work of the future become increasingly grounded in theory and research (LaCrosse, 1986)?

This chapter also discusses the ways student affairs professional associations can meet the needs of the more seasoned student affairs administrators who have found their curiosity dampened and energy for research drained by the press of administrative duties. For these student affairs workers, continuing education opportunities sponsored by national professional associations can provide needed guidance and support for meeting the "calls to assessment" of campus environments that keep getting "curiouser and curiouser!"

Isn't It Curious!

"Curiouser and curiouser!" cried Alice (she was so much surprised that for the moment she quite forgot how to speak good English).

Alice's Adventures in Wonderland
Chapter II: The Pool of Tears

Like Wonderland, campus environments can certainly be described as curious and intriguing. Student affairs professionals work daily in environments conducive to wonder and discovery. College and university campuses are characterized by questioning and exploration in which all members of the academy participate as partners in learning. Interestingly enough, however, graduate students entering higher education and student affairs receive mixed and confusing messages about research and data gathering. Even prior to enrolling in graduate programs, these new members of the profession have no doubt grappled with math anxiety, and stellar performance on the quantitative or analytic sections of the Graduate Record Examination is not the norm among preparation program applicants (Young, 1986). Probably not exposed to qualitative or naturalistic research methods as undergraduates, new graduate students have only limited experience with empirical research, often from statistics courses taken as college sophomores, to frame their opinions about inquiry activities. Like new graduate students in other behavioral sciences (Gelso, Raphael & Black, 1983), new students enrolling in higher education preparation programs may equate research only with statistics, thus dampening enthusiasm for inquiry activities. The powerful effect of early negative experiences with research and statistics contributes to new students' preferences for subsequent roles as administrators rather than scholars. Before they enter graduate school or confront the research of the field, new members of the profession have often formed opinions that research is a "frustrating and tiresome activity" (Holland, 1986, p. 123).

Graduate students entering preparation programs in higher education and student affairs administration encounter even more curiosities. Since most of the profession's graduate preparation programs are in large research-oriented universities, new master's degree students are likely to witness: (a) doctoral students grumbling about hurdles encountered during dissertation research; (b) new faculty emoting anxiety about institutional expectations for research and publication productivity needed for tenure; (c) assistantship and practicum supervisors not current in research who place low priority on programmatic inquiry or assessment activities (McEwen & Shertzer, 1975); and (d) little contact with those faculty members who genuinely enjoy research and inquiry activities. Add to that the advice of well-meaning mentors that prospective employers do not rate coursework in research or evaluation as valuable to satisfactory job performance (Ostroth, 1975) and it is curious indeed that recipients of graduate degrees in higher education and student affairs programs ever display any interest in research at all! Yet what could be more important than designing graduate curricula which address the pressing need for the profession to develop skilled producers and users of information (Brown, 1985)?

Calming the Terrors

Alice soon came to the conclusion that it was a very difficult game indeed. The players all played at once, without waiting for turns, quarreling all the while . . . and in a very short time the Queen was in a furious passion and went

stamping about and shouting, "Off with his head!" or "Off
with her head!"

   Alice began to feel very uneasy; to be sure, she had not as
yet had any dispute with the Queen, but she knew that it
might happen, any minute, "and then," thought she, "what
would become of me?"

Alice's Adventures in Wonderland
Chapter VIII: The Queen's Croquet Ground

Fears about "what would become of me" are common among
student affairs graduate students encountering curricular
standards for research competence. Of course anxiety
about expectations for research is not unique to graduate
students in higher education and student affairs. Difficulties
in overcoming hurdles of research are documented by the
large number of graduate students across many disciplines
who "stall out" after their coursework is completed and remain "ABD" (all but dissertation), anguish over the research for their dissertations, or if graduated, never again
engage in research (Frank, 1986). The stresses encountered by graduate students in higher education and student
affairs are not unique, and their research orientations probably do not lag behind those of students in other fields (Kuh,
Lardy & Greenlee, 1979). However, it is not enough to know
that other disciplines share similar difficulties with regard
to graduate student anxieties over research, "for an attitude
of 'misery loves company' should not be a profession's
credo, either" (Cesari, 1986, p. 153).

   Fortunately, studies of the process by which dispositions
toward research are developed indicate that the more
graduate students are exposed to research and participate
in inquiry activities, the more likely they are to strengthen
their research orientations and find these activities satisfy-
ing (Hunter & Kuh, 1987; Kuh, Lardy & Greenlee, 1979;
Worthen & Roaden, 1975). Students' anxieties as to "what
would become of me?" abate when they work with enthu-
siastic faculty to experience both the challenges and joys

inherent in the promise and practice of research applied to their profession. The key appears to be aiding graduate students in achieving early successes with research activities (Hunter & Kuh, 1987) by setting expectations that inquiry is a critical professional function and by structuring opportunities to develop dispositions favorable to research.

Opportunities to experience success with research might stem from course assignments requiring original inquiry activities or developing research proposals, research assistantships, or other collaboration with more experienced researchers on projects leading to conference presentations or publications. These successes have an "accumulative effect" (Clark & Corcoran, 1986, p. 20) which sparks confidence in and identification with research endeavors. If faculty create opportunities for students to plan, conduct, and report research, students are more likely to conclude, "Maybe I don't dislike research after all. I'm doing it, aren't I?" (Cesari, 1986, p. 156).

Suggestions for enhancing the research orientations of graduate students in higher education and student affairs can be found in the literature on faculty research productivity. Studies of factors affiliated with the research productivity of faculty across many disciplines conclude that institutional expectations and rewards for research (i.e., promotion, tenure, merit pay), and the influence of productive colleagues, combine to promote favorable socialization of new faculty toward research (Blackburn, 1985; Braxton, 1983; Lawrence & Blackburn, 1985). These findings suggest that whether the research orientations of graduate students in student affairs are repressed or encouraged would similarly depend on programmatic expectations and available support, combined with the behaviors and attitudes of their student peers (Blau, 1973).

Unfortunately, graduate programs in student affairs seldom provide the type of institutional support for their students' research that is available to graduate students in other disciplines. For example, 62.5 percent of the graduate programs in counseling psychology provided travel funds for graduate students presenting research at professional meetings; 48.6 percent provided typing services for students' research manuscripts; 43.2 percent sponsored monthly seminars to discuss research (Galassi, Brooks, Stoltz & Trexler, 1986). If the profession of higher education and student affairs seek to promote the research orientations of those entering the profession, then graduate preparation program faculty must play influential roles. Beginning with the recruitment materials they distribute to applicants, and continuing with the curricular expectations they communicate, and extending to the research opportunities and support they provide, faculty must set clear expectations to the graduate students enrolled in their programs.

Tips for the Tortoise

"When we were little," the Mock Turtle went on, "We went to school in the sea. The Master was an old Turtle—we used to call him Tortoise."

"Why did you call him Tortoise, if he wasn't one?" Alice asked.

"We called him Tortoise because he taught us," said the Mock Turtle angrily.

Alice's Adventures in Wonderland
Chapter IX: The Mock Turtle's Story

Graduates of preparation programs in higher education and student affairs can point to many things that faculty have "taught" them. Faculty affiliated with these preparation programs are charged with the far-reaching responsibilities of socializing new members to their professional roles and aiding them in developing the knowledge and competence important for their advancement within the profession. Socialization during graduate school includes the process by which students acquire the "values, attitudes, norms, knowledge, and skills needed to perform their roles" (Bragg, 1976, p. 7). Unfortunately, the number of faculty who identify with higher education or student affairs as their field of activity is very small within any graduate program (ACPA, 1987). Frequently "two or three persons, sometimes only one, will carry the program" (Cooper, 1980, p. 31). For this reason, student affairs faculty face complex and diverse challenges as they structure comprehensive curricula to educate and socialize entering members of the profession.

Because graduate curricula in student affairs are expected to prepare graduates to be "experts on students and their environments" (NASPA, 1987, p. 14), the educational program, including classroom instruction, practica internships and paid assistantships, must be comprehensive and well coordinated. Debate continues about the appropriate balance between students' expected mastery of the profession's knowledge base and students' acquisition of necessary skills and competencies needed for professional practice (Hymen, 1988; Meabon & Owens, 1984). Curricula responsive to professional expectations and employers' needs currently include a mixture of philosophy and history of student affairs as well as student development, organizational theory, campus ecology, and counseling and intervention strategies (ACPA, 1987).

While little guidance is available to preparation faculty to aid them in structuring what graduates should know (Hunter & Comey, in press), the expectation that graduates possess competence in research and evaluation has been clearly stated. The 1986 graduate program guidelines published by the Council for the Advancement of Standards (CAS, 1986) indicated that "central to the basis of the (preparation) program must be the spirit and practice of inquiry and the production and use of research, evaluation and assessment data by faculty and students" (p. 104).

Although clearly a priority for curricula design, developing research competence among graduate students is not a simple task for faculty in any discipline. The most common complaint among faculty affiliated with graduate programs in journalism was the lack of undergraduate preparation for research, which dictated that graduate research courses be "watered down and nonthreatening" (Fowler, 1986, p. 598). No correlation has been found between the number of courses taken in research methodology and subsequent research productivity; therefore, simply adding the requirement of a research methodology course is not sufficient. What is needed are incorporating processes by which new members of the profession can be socialized to the roles of inquiry and research as integral to their preparation for professional practice in student affairs.

Studies of socialization in graduate schools highlight the importance of faculty in influencing students in their orientations toward research (LaCrosse, 1986). The suggestion is that preparation program faculty and the climate of the graduate program are powerful influences on both the career development of student affairs workers and their orientations toward research. Toward this end, the following questions serve as guides for faculty who wish to structure curricula to maximize the development of research competence among graduate students in either master's or doctoral programs in higher education and student affairs:

1. Are the program faculty clear in their commitment to fostering students' research orientations and skills?

2. Do the recruitment materials distributed by the graduate program communicate expectations that all graduates will possess research competencies?

3. Do the curricular requirements include coursework in inquiry methodology in student affairs which familiarizes all students with both qualitative and quantitative inquiry paradigms?

4. Are students expected in each class in their curricula to engage in original research projects which bear on issues, questions, theories, and professional practices?

5. Do class assignments for each class include assignments like developing research proposals or applications for research grants?

6. Does the graduate program sponsor a professional journal for which students serve as editorial board members and authors of articles of their original research?

7. Do semester-long practica internships include opportunities for student and supervisor to frame research questions of relevance to practice?

8. Does the graduate program require the completion of an original piece of research as a requirement for completion of the degree?

9. Does the graduate program sponsor a "colloquium" series by which campus student affairs practitioners and students can present their research and findings to colleagues?

10. Do interested students have the opportunity to collaborate with more experienced researchers (i.e., practitioners or faculty) on inquiry projects?

11. Does the graduate program demonstrate a developmental approach to sparking and nurturing the research orientations of all students?

12. Are all members of the faculty affiliated with the graduate program (i.e., teaching faculty, practica supervisors, assistantship employers) in partnership in the task of fostering research orientations?

13. Are all graduates competent in computer applications to student affairs work?

14. Are all students acquainted with the institutional studies efforts on the campus to assess student outcomes?

15. Has the graduate program established cooperative agreements with student affairs practitioners by which students have access to data collection on the campus?

Brown (1985) asked the profession whether it is possible to design a training program based on an ideal. While developing research competencies among all graduates of preparation programs stands at present as ideal, achieving this goal is critical in order for the profession to advance in its scholarship and professional practice. Additional benefits of increased research practices can be expected from the increased credibility of student affairs workers with other faculty throughout the institution (Saddlemire, 1988). The stakes are high; however, preparation program faculty cannot socialize new members of the student affairs profession toward research with the mere addition of a research course. Curricular requirements alone will not substitute for opportunities for firsthand experience in shaping "curiosities" into questions amenable to scholarly inquiry.

The promise held by the practice of student affairs research can be advanced through partnerships among preparation program faculty and other student affairs practitioners on the campus. For student affairs workers already employed in the field, professional associations must join the partnership to assist members to perform their roles in campus environments which are increasingly emphasizing assessment and research.

Professional Associations and Continuing Education

"Aren't you sometimes frightened at being planted out here, with nobody to care for you?" asked Alice.

"There's the tree in the middle," said the Rose. "What else is it good for?"

"But what could it do, if any danger came?" Alice asked.

"It could bark," said the Rose.

"It says 'bough-wough!'" cried a Daisy. "That's why its branches are called boughs!"

Alice's Adventures in Wonderland
Chapter II: The Garden of Live Flowers

Once graduated from their master's degree preparation programs in student affairs, student affairs workers may look around at the "curious" environments of their campuses and find themselves "frightened at being planted out [t]here, with nobody to care for [them]." While alumni networks remain strong and links with preparation program faculty are nurtured for many graduates, student affairs professionals may feel isolated and anxious as they struggle to make sense of their work places or to assess the effectiveness of their efforts. It is evidence of the "curious" nature of human beings that student affairs professionals can support so enthusiastically the lifelong education of their students yet be bashful about continuing their own education beyond their graduate degree programs (Penn & Trow, 1987). Members of the student affairs profession tend to "do what they do best or are most familiar with" (Miller, 1988, p. 117), and are therefore likely to resist challenges that are too imposing or threatening. However, the profession cannot resist the press for research and assessment, waiting endlessly for new members to complete their graduate preparation programs with newly acquired research competencies. Of the student affairs divisions surveyed, 29 percent employ no staff trained in doing research (Johnson & Steele, 1984). Those student affairs workers currently employed in the field must also acquire research and assessment skills through professional development and continuing education activities.

Learning how to do research requires practice and guidance, and members of the profession need to be able to design studies and have them reviewed by seasoned and supportive researchers (Frank, 1986). For those who find themselves "frightened at being planted out [t]here with nobody to care for [them]" the student affairs professional associations can provide the "bark" with which to keep danger at bay. While the responsibility for engaging in professional development and continuing education rests with the individual members of the profession (Creamer, 1988), professional associations can provide the necessary support for student affairs workers to acquire and improve the skills and competencies needed for research.

Professional associations affiliated with student affairs are in the powerful position to link student affairs workers who vary in terms of seniority, functional areas, institutional settings, or geography. The National Association of Student Personnel Administrators (NASPA), the American College Personnel Association (ACPA), and the National Association for Women Deans, Administrators and Counselors (NAWDAC) have total memberships of approximately 14,550 (Hunter, 1989). Through scholarly journals, national conferences, and regional workshops these associations support continuing professional education by disseminating current information and stimulating the exchange of ideas among colleagues. Professional education stands as the "primary purpose" of these associations (Schrank & Young, 1987, p. 65). Accordingly, professional associations can be instrumental in promoting an ethos of inquiry and supporting members' efforts to strengthen research competencies. Toward this end, the following questions can guide the efforts of professional associations to rekindle members' orientations toward research and fuel the development of competence in research:

1. Is the professional association willing to commit itself to taking a leadership role in sparking, developing, and rewarding members' research orientations and competence?

2. How is the association fostering an ethos of inquiry among members?

3. What opportunities (i.e., preconference workshops, regional institutes, etc.) does the association provide for members to acquire the research and assessment skills they need?

4. Does the association provide sections within its scholarly journal reserved for "first authors" to attract the scholarship of a wider group of professionals?

5. Does the association provide competitions for research funding for which practitioners are not competing with faculty who may be functioning at a higher level of research competence?

6. Does the professional association sponsor graduate student "case study competitions" in which student teams are challenged to develop assessment plans to meet simulated scenarios?

7. Does the association sponsor graduate student research awards in addition to Dissertation of the Year Awards or sponsor research proposal competitions for recent graduates of preparation programs?

8. How can the association make research meaningful to members who are unskilled in applying research findings in their professional practice?

9. Does the association sponsor or coordinate a network for researchers using available technology (e.g., BITNET, FAX) for sharing literature, reports, research designs, instruments, etc.?

10. What does the association do to promote high quality research and evaluation in conducting its own business?

Anticipation

"Take care of yourself!" screamed the White Queen, seizing Alice's hair with both hands. "Something's going to happen!"

And then all sorts of things happened in a moment. There was not a moment to be lost. At any other time Alice would have felt surprised, but she was far too much excited to be surprised at anything now.

Alice's Adventures in Wonderland
Chapter IX: Queen Alice

Student affairs administrators today work in settings in which "all sorts of things" are happening. They work in very curious environments in which the education of members of the profession has included such sage advice as "expect disorder and don't panic" (Kuh, 1983, p. 76). In light of recent calls for more widespread participation in research and assessment, student affairs workers today would also be encouraged to realize "that in working on a campus everything should be recognized as potential data" (Reinharz, 1979, p. 152). Therefore, both student affairs preparation programs and professional associations must set the standard that "inquiring minds want to know!" They must examine their expectations and practices regarding the preparation of new student affairs workers and support established practitioners as they acquire or sharpen the skills needed to embark on research activities (Ford, 1975). Only then will campus Wonderlands be more fully understood, effectively managed, and educationally improved.

References

ACPA (1987). *Directory of graduate preparation programs in college student personnel.* Alexandria, VA: American College Personnel Association.

Blackburn, R.T. (1985). Faculty career development: Theory and practice. In S. Clark and D. Lewis (eds.), *Faculty vitality and institutional productivity* (pp. 55-85). New York: Teachers College Press.

Blau, P.M. (1973). *The organization of academic work.* New York: Wiley.

Bragg, A.K. (1976). *The socialization process in higher education.* ERIC/Higher Education Research Report No. 7. Washington, DC: American Association for Higher Education.

Braxton, J.M. (1983). Department colleagues and individual faculty publication productivity. *The Review of Higher Education* 6(2), 115-28.

Brown, R.D. (1972). *Student development in tomorrow's education: A return to the academy.* Washington, DC: American Personnel and Guidance Association.

Brown, R.D. (1985). Graduate education for the student development educator: A content and process model. *NASPA Journal,* 22, 38-43.

CAS (1986). *CAS standards and guidelines for student services/development programs.* Washington, DC: ACT.

Cesari, J.P. (1986). Research training: More questions than answers. *The Counseling Psychologist,* 14(1), 153-57.

Clark, S.M., and Corcoran, M. (1986). Perspectives on the professional socialization of women faculty: A case of accumulative disadvantage? *Journal of Higher Education,* 57(1), 20-43.

Cooper, J.H. (1980). Special problems of the professor of higher education. *The Review of Higher Education,* 4(1), 25-32.

Creamer, D.G. (1988). A model of in-service education: Professional initiative for continuous learning. In R.B. Young and L.V. Moore (eds.), *The state of the art of professional education and practice.* Alexandria, VA: American College Personnel Association.

Ford, J. (1975). *Paradigms and fairy tales.* Boston: Routledge and Kegan Paul.

Fowler, G.L. (1986). Content and teacher characteristics for master's level research course. *Journalism Quarterly,* 63, 594-99.

Frank, G. (1986). The "Boulder Model" revisited: The training of the clinical psychologist for research. *Psychological Reports,* 58, 579-85.

Galassi, J.P.; Brooks, L.; Stoltz, R.F.; and Trexler, K.A. (1986). Research training environments and student productivity: An exploratory study. *The Counseling Psychologist,* 14(1), 31-36.

Gelso, C.J.; Raphael, R.; Black, S.M. (1983). Research training in counseling psychology: Some preliminary data. *Journal of Counseling Psychology,* 30, 611-14.

Gottlieb, D. (1961). Processes of socialization in American graduate schools. *Social Forces,* 40, 124-31.

Holland, J.L. (1986). Student selection, training, and research performance. *The Counseling Psychologist,* 14(1), 121-25.

Hunter, D.E. (1989). Knowledge dissemination at professional conferences: Women's ways of sharing. *Initiatives,* 52(2), 15-23.

Hunter, D.E., and Comey, D. (in press). Common learning in student affairs. *NASPA Journal.*

Hunter, D.E., and Kuh, G.D. (1987). The write-wing: Prolific contributors to the higher education and student affairs literature. *Journal of Higher Education,* 58(4), 443-62.

Hymen, R.E. (1988). Graduate preparation for professional practice: A difference of perceptions. *NASPA Journal,* 26(2), 143-50.

Johnson, D.H., and Steele, B.H. (1984). A national survey of research activity and attitudes in student affairs divisions. *Journal of College Student Personnel,* 25(3), 200-05.

Kuh, G.D. (1979). Building a wolf-proof house: Integrating evaluation in student affairs. In G.D. Kuh, (ed.), *Evaluation in student affairs.* Cincinnati: American College Personnel Association.

Kuh, G.D. (1983). Tactics for understanding and improving student affairs organizations. In G.D. Kuh (ed.), *Understanding student affairs organizations.* New Directions for Student Services. San Francisco: Jossey-Bass Publisher, Inc.

Kuh, G.D.; Lardy, B.A.; and Greenlee, F.E. (1979). Research orientation of graduate students in college student personnel. *Journal of College Student Personnel,* 20, 99-104.

LaCrosse, M.B. (1986). Research training: In search of a human science. *The Counseling Psychologist,* 14(1), 147-51.

Lawrence, J.H., and Blackburn, R.T. (1985). Faculty careers: Maturation, demographic, and historical effects. *Research in Higher Education,* 22, 135-54.

McEwen, M., and Shertzer, B. (1975). An analysis of certain attitudes and beliefs among the memberships of ACPA, NASPA, and NAWDAC. *Journal of College Student Personnel,* 16, 190-94.

Meabon, D.L., and Owens, H.F. (1984). Graduate preparation programs in college student personnel: The introductory course. *NASPA Journal,* 22(1), 2-12.

Miller, T.K. (1988). Challenge, support, and response: An

epilogue. In R.B. Young and L.V. Moore (eds.), *The state of the art of professional education and practice.* Alexandria, VA: American College Personnel Association.

NASPA (1987). *A perspective on student affairs.* Washington, DC: National Association of Student Personnel Administrators.

Ostroth, D.D. (1975). Master's level preparation for student personnel work. *Journal of College Student Personnel,* 16, 319-22.

Penn, J.R., and Trow, J. (1987). Expanding graduate education. In L.V. Moore and R.B. Young (eds.), *Expanding opportunities for professional education.* New Directions for Student Services, No. 37. San Francisco: Jossey-Bass Publisher, Inc.

Reinharz, S. (1979). *On becoming a social scientist.* San Francisco: Jossey-Bass Publisher, Inc.

Saddlemire, G. (1988). Designing a curriculum for student services/development professionals. In R.B. Young and L.V. Moore (eds.), *The state of the art of professional education and practice.* Alexandria, VA: American College Personnel Association

Schrank, M., and Young, R.B. (1987). The role of professional associations. In L.V. Moore and R.B. Young (eds.), *Expanding opportunities for professional education.* New Directions for Student Services, No. 37. San Francisco: Jossey-Bass Publisher, Inc.

Worthen, B.R., and Roaden, A.L. (1975). *The research assistantship: Recommendations for colleges and universities.* Bloomington, IN: Phi Delta Kappa.

Young, R.B. (1986). An exploratory study of admissions information and success in a preparation program for student personnel workers. *Journal of College Student Personnel,* 27(2), 131-36.

Young, R.B. (1987). A model of professional education. In L.V. Moore and R.B. Young (eds.), *Expanding opportunities for professional education.* New Directions for Student Services, No. 37. San Francisco: Jossey-Bass Publisher, Inc.

Chapter 7

Student Affairs Research on Trial

Robert D. Brown

"I'll be judge, I'll be jury," said cunning old Fury.
"I'll try the whole cause, and condemn you to death."
Alice's Adventures in Wonderland
Chapter III: A Caucus-Race and a Long Tale

Nearly 25 years ago in an American College Personnel Association presidential speech, Ralph Berdie (1966) proposed that the profession use the behavioral scientist model as the framework for training and practice in student personnel work. He noted that for him, "Student personnel work is the application in higher education of knowledge and principles derived from the social and behavioral sciences, particularly from psychology, educational psychology, and sociology" (p. 146). He characterized the student personnel worker as "the behavioral scientist whose subject matter is the student and whose sociopsychological sphere is the college" (p. 146).

Berdie suggested that professionals in student affairs need to think and act like scientists as they work with students. More recently, the term scientist-practitioner has been used to refer to this model. It describes not so much what scientist-practitioners do as how they go about what they do. Scientist-practitioners are professionals who bring scientific principles to bear in their everyday practice. An essential activity of being "scientific" is using research as an aid in making decisions that are a daily part of a practitioner's life. Past experience and intuition are important, but scientist-practitioners look for objective confirmation of their perceptions and base their decisions on more than their own best hunches. Being scientific is not exclusively equated with conducting experiments or using high powered statistics. It is creating and operating within a environment that the editors of this monograph and others refer to as an "ethos of inquiry" (see Hunter & Beeler, Chapter Six). It means asking such questions as:

- Why is this working or not working? This involves searching for an explanation or a theory.
- What have other people found in similar situations? This would mean examining past research.
- How can we improve what we are doing? This involves constructing hypotheses and conducting evaluations.

Do student affairs professionals practice in such an environment? Is the amount and quality of research student affairs professionals conduct and how they think about it and use it sufficient for these professionals to be considered scientist-practitioners?

In this chapter, I am putting student affairs research on trial. Like old Fury, I am serving as both judge and jury. I do not believe the profession has made sufficient progress toward achieving the scientist-practitioner model as a norm for behavior. Until the scientist-practitioner model becomes a fuller reality the profession, higher education, and, most important, the students will suffer. In this chapter, I will share with you why I arrived at this conclusion and what must be done to start the profession on a path to making the scientist-practitioner model the rule rather than the exception.

Perspective

Before the trial begins, let me first preface my comments with this caveat. As a profession and as individuals, student affairs members are probably not much behind other applied fields of the social and behavioral sciences in failing to fulfill the scientist-practitioner idea. Colleagues in the counseling field aspire to the same model and may even talk about the model more than student affairs professionals do, but they still have far to go in making it a practical reality (Meara, 1990).

Certainly, faculty colleagues in higher education are remiss in applying research findings and theory about learning and instruction in their own instructional practice. Many do not even pretend to make such an application a significant part of their responsibilities. Other helping professions (e.g., social workers) are by no means ahead of student affairs in making this model a reality. I make these comments about other professions to place student affairs in perspective, not to make student affairs professionals feel better. Student affairs professionals have enough excuses for not measuring up (see Benedict, Chapter Two) and I do not want to add to them. It is quite possible that other professions are trying harder to promote the scientist-practitioner ideal, while we in student affairs are still talking about it.

Charges against the Current Status of Student Affairs Research

"Write that down," the King said to the jury, and the jury eagerly wrote down all three dates on their slates, and then added them up, and reduced the answer to shillings and pence.

Alice's Adventures in Wonderland
Chapter IX: The Mock Turtle's Story

What are the charges against student affairs research? Of what crimes is it accused? Here are the charges:

Too few persons are doing quality research. At the risk of being rash, I estimate that there are no more than a half dozen persons in the country doing quality research that relates to the profession directly or even indirectly. I suggest that there are not more than another half dozen persons associated with the profession who could be called theorists. Too many of the theorists are advancing propositions based on unrepresentative samples or on data collected years ago. That makes six researchers and six theorists—an even dozen. If pressed, considering that several are not really members of the student affairs profession, I could easily trim that down to eight. That is not enough to sustain a roster of role models and mentors.

Administrators fail to be models for the scientist-practitioner role. A major responsibility for making the scientist-practitioner model a reality rests with campus administrators. The excuse that "there isn't enough time" is a myth, as Benedict suggested in Chapter Two. Many administrators place a higher premium on attending to campus political issues than to student affairs research. They fail to recognize the value of research as a political tool. Research needs to be on the list of essential activities. I know several major student affairs administrators who actively pursue scholarly activities related directly to their administrative duties, and even a few who do so on issues not so directly related to their duties. How do these few administrators do it? Are they remarkably blessed with unusual talents? Do their campuses have fewer of the proverbial "fires" to put out? I do not think so. My guess is that they are well-organized, set appropriate priorities, and realize that applying science to their profession makes them more effective.

Overreliance on surveys. I have not conducted a count, but my guess is that 90 percent of the research articles submitted for publication in student affairs journals are surveys and about 80 percent of the published articles are based on survey research. Now, survey research has its place. There are times when it is informative to know who is doing what, when, how, and to whom. Sometimes, it is even helpful to know whether different people are now doing whatever, however, and to whomever more or less than they were a decade ago. But student affairs researchers are much too quick to turn to the survey as a research methodology. Too often the publication of survey results either locally on the college campus or in a journal leads to nothing more than a few comments like "Isn't that interesting?" and nothing else happens. The researchers go on to their next survey and only return to the topic again when they think it is timely to compare this decade with the last decade.

Too much atheoretical research. Much of what passes for research in student affairs is what I refer to as "I-was-walking-on-campus-one-day" research or "I-was-wondering-what-if" research. The full scenario goes something like this: "I was walking on campus one day when suddenly I wondered if students who wear running shoes to classes take their education less seriously than students who wear traditional dress shoes. I wonder if there is a relationship between types of shoes students wear and their attitude toward college?" Curiosity and real life issues are excellent starting points for valuable research questions, but too often the student affairs researcher leaps directly from the "I wonder what if" inspiration to construction of a questionnaire without relating the question to a theoretical premise about the matter, without checking to see what previous research has been done on this topic, and without thinking about whether the answer to the question serves any other purpose than to satisfy curiosity.

Too much amoral research. Much of student affairs research is intended to help professionals understand students. But researchers fail too often to ask themselves whether their study has any moral purpose or value. Is the research question clearly focused on an important issue? Too often, the answer is "No." Are the results useful for some decision that must be made about student life? Too often, the answer is "No." Is the researcher planning to

follow up the results of the survey with a planned intervention to improve the situation? Almost always, the answer is
"No."

In my judgment, if the answer to any one of these three
questions is "No," then the research serves no moral purpose. And, if the answer to at least two of the three questions
is "No," then I might even consider the research effort im-
moral, especially if it means that the data collection process
is going to take up considerable amounts (more than 10
minutes) of any person's time.

Doing qualitative research for the wrong reasons. I support
much of what has been said in previous chapters regarding
the need for more qualitative research studies (see Kuh,
Chapter Four). Indeed, even though I was born and raised
with quantitative and experimental research, I have been
using and stressing the need for qualitative research for two
decades (Brown, 1972), have illustrated various qualitative
research methods in the interim (Brown, 1978), and have
reiterated the need for more qualitative research in my first
editorial in the *Journal of College Student Personnel* (Brown,
1983). Despite being one of those pointing the way before
the bandwagon had its wheels on, I want to caution those
jumping on the paradigm shift bandwagon. Paradigm
shifters need to be aware of unintended negative side effects
of their efforts. A sizeable group of people join the qualitative
research troops because they "never liked numbers."
These are people who see qualitative research as being less
rigorous or demanding. These are often people who "hate
statistics." I worry about people who go in one direction
primarily because they are fearful of what lies in the other
direction. If they are not willing to extend the effort to try to
understand moderately sophisticated analyses, I fear they
will not be willing to extend the effort to conduct good
qualitative research. I fear that when these same people
conduct qualitative studies, they will produce shoddy
studies that will give the approach a bad name. This could
easily result in a backlash and instead of a paradigm shift,

there will be a paradigm swing or a paradigm pendulum. Quantitative research has not been tried and found wanting; rather it has not been truly tried.

Too many grade prediction studies. As far as I am concerned, you can read the grade prediction studies from first to last (indeed, the paper they are written on must be enough to build a papier-mache tower to the moon! and back!), and you can distill their worth to maybe two to three articles. I am tired of reading that this or that variable adds one-one hundredth of a percent of accuracy to the grade prediction equation. So what!

Much the same could be said about retention studies. If an equal amount of energy, time, and money went into improving the quality of instruction and life on campuses as goes into so-called enrollment management studies, retention would not be a major concern.

Researchers conducting grade prediction studies are similar to those conducting surveys. They go from project to project examining different, often esoteric, variables that might be related to grades. If they can, they examine the value of their prediction equation for students in one college and then another, for students in one major and then another, and for students of one ethnic background and then another. They seldom, however, stop to assess the impact programmatic changes might have on grades or retention rates. Their results may provide clues as to who the high-risk students are likely to be, but they do not take the next step to find out what intervention strategies might help these high-risk students succeed.

Missing the outcome assessment movement. The outcome assessment movement in higher education may well come and go before student affairs wakes up and responds to the challenges and opportunities. In Chapter Five, Hanson noted that faculty and academic administrators on campus can be helped if student affairs staffs will assume important roles in making the right information available and understandable to them. The call for accountability that provoked elementary and secondary educators to rethink their goals and instructional practices has at least resulted in much debate. It is higher education's turn and student affairs has an important stake and I believe an important role in determining what happens.

Who is Guilty and What is the Sentence?

"No! No! Sentence first—verdict afterwards."

Alice's Adventures in Wonderland
Chapter XII: Alice's Evidence

Since I am serving as judge and jury, I can skip the verdict and go directly from the charges to the sentence. Earlier chapters pinpointed actions that might be taken by persons and groups involved in student affairs ranging from faculty in preparation programs to professional associations. I support all the preceding suggestions. I would like to highlight a few and add a few. My answer to the question, "Who is guilty?" is primarily the campus administrators, but first I will comment briefly about preparation programs and professional associations.

Preparation Programs

As Hunter and Beeler noted in Chapter Six, both the NASPA (1987) statement and the CAS standards (1986) suggest that training in inquiry methods must be important dimensions of professional preparation programs. Hunter and Beeler also appropriately noted that having students take research courses is not likely to dramatically add to the students' skill levels or, even more important, increase their self-confidence in conducting research. What students need, according to Hunter and Beeler, is more firsthand experience. I agree, but at the same time I have concerns about where they are going to get this experience and what the quality of that experience will be.

Many faculty in student development and student services preparation programs are former practitioners them-

selves. Many have the same love-hate relationship to research which Hunter and Beeler ascribed to the service-
oriented practitioner. Being faculty members may force
them to conduct research so they will be promoted and at-
tain tenure, but this does not guarantee they will like it or
that what they do is good research. Will this mean students
will collaborate with faculty on more surveys? Will this mean
more grade prediction studies? Will this mean more surveys
on the needs of nontraditional students, women students, or
international students (you name your favorite student sub-
population) without any follow-up programming to meet
those needs or studies to determine the most effective intervention strategies to meet those needs? Will this mean
more studies on alcohol abuse, drug usage, at-risk sexual
activities, or hazing behavior (you name your issues) without any research on the effectiveness of programs or policies to eliminate the behavior?

Students must be socialized into the value of conducting
research as part of their professional life, but I hope the
socialization process incorporates the necessity of using
quality research to address important issues in student life
and student development. Student affairs does not need
more research as an end in itself; it needs more useful, high
quality research.

The link between the researcher and the practitioner is
weak and often nonexistent. I have puzzled over this issue in
other arenas, including counselor and teacher education.
No easy solution exists. Some suggest the researcher needs
to collaborate with the practitioner in deciding what research questions to ask and how to conduct the research.
Maybe that is asking too much of both. Usually researchers
stumble over their own feet when they leave their arrogance
behind and try to collaborate. And, I am not sure that
practitioners know how to ask good research questions.
This is where continuing education workshops sponsored
by preparation programs might help.

Practitioners must be bold and persistent in demanding that faculty in preparation programs conduct meaningful research, and faculty in preparation programs must not be timid in helping practitioners frame questions and bring theory to bear on practical problems. Certainly, this is a place where expertise in program evaluation and qualitative methods (see Kuh, Chapter Four) and efficient use of time and economical approaches such as focus groups (see Weitzer & Malaney, Chapter Three) might help bridge the gap.

Professional Associations

Professional associations also have a role to play in encouraging research, according to Hunter and Beeler (see Chapter Six). I agree and I also believe that professional associations have been reasonably responsive in supporting research projects and sponsoring awards such as those for best dissertation project. Having chaired the awards committee for one association and having seen the awards made by others, however, I have to admit candidly that I have never been overwhelmed by the number of nominations or the quality of the products submitted. I hope the fault lies in too few nominations being made rather than the quality of the efforts being poor overall. Certainly, the professional associations cannot be faulted for trying.

I have two suggestions for professional associations, relative to their annual conventions and to their journals. My recommendations are closely related and they both focus on stressing quality, even if it means reducing quantity. Let me speak about ACPA's convention because that it is one with which I am most familiar. There is something to be said for having many programs scheduled; it gives more professionals an opportunity to make presentations and it gives attenders more program selections to choose. It certainly encourages fuller attendance and participation. However, it does so at the cost of quality of the average program.

If you were to categorize convention presentations as to whether they were theory-based, entailed data beyond anecdotes, and included prepared papers, you would find too many that were atheoretical, seeped in anecdotes, and with no formal paper or handouts. Convention paper selection criteria should include requiring presentation of data related to the effectiveness of the campus projects and innovations being described, having an honest critique by an independent discussant after each presentation, and requiring presenters to have formal papers available at the convention and by mail to professionals who cannot attend the convention. These stipulations might reduce the number of presentations by a third, but I think shortly the presentation proposals would match these criteria and I strongly believe the overall quality would rise significantly.

Much the same could be said about professional journals. There are not enough good research articles to fill the professional journals. Professional association journals could easily reduce the number of pages published without reducing the value of information shared. In six years as editor of the *Journal of College Student Personnel/Development,* I like to think I never recommended any manuscript for publication that did not merit publication. I think the journal publishes research articles of high quality. I would be less than honest with myself, however, if I did not acknowledge that my standards could (or maybe should) have been raised a notch or two. Though less familiar with the manuscript submissions, I feel comfortable in saying the same for other professional journals in student affairs, past and present. Maybe the journals should be quarterlies instead of bimonthlies, or biannuals instead of quarterlies. Maybe several associations could jointly publish a journal.

Having fewer journal pages would not directly result in higher quality research in the field. But by doing so, the journals would have a higher standard and provide models for excellence in research. If this action was taken only as an isolated response to this monograph and my comments, it would do little to reduce the fear that students and new professionals have about research. I would hope that journal editors and professional associations will continue to provide workshops and forums, and other means for research neophytes to overcome their fears and gain confidence.

Campus Administrators

Though the preparation programs and professional associations can be supportive of efforts to increase the quantity of research and its quality, I believe their resources are limited, as well as their influence. I think the real challenge lies in the hands of campus administrators. Even if preparation programs place a strong emphasis on research and graduate new professionals who have excellent skills and are excited about research, if new professionals are not reinforced and supported for being involved in research on the job, the skills will rust away from disuse and the excitement will turn to cynicism. A decade ago, Kuh, Lardy and Greenlee (1979) reported that students in their study exhibited a relatively strong research orientation, but the authors warned that research in the field would not increase unless these same students were supported by their professional colleagues. I doubt that they have been.

I think the persons who can change this pattern significantly are the vice presidents and vice chancellors for student affairs. Changes in preparation programs and professional associations may make dents, but chief student affairs officers are in a position to remodel the entire professions' orientation toward research. Chief student affairs officers do not have to look far for directions, guidelines, and examples of how programmatic research and evaluation can be implemented to help them make decisions about their programs. In Chapter Three, Weitzer and Malaney presented examples of economical ways to implement a research agenda on campus. Moxley (1988) described how a central research office can facilitate and promote research. I have presented examples of how counseling centers (Brown, 1987), advising programs (Brown & Sanstead, 1982), and learning centers (Brown, 1980) can be evaluated.

Kuh's (1980) work on evaluation has been available for over a decade.

The tough question is why these resources have not been fully utilized. A recent report by Beeler and Oblander (1989) does not present a brighter picture than that provided by Johnson and Steele (1984). Such adjectives as "moderate," "little," and "very little" are the most prominent descriptors of the quantity of studies. Neither the Beeler-Oblander study nor Johnson-Steele study directly addressed questions about the quality of the research being conducted in student affairs, but Beeler and Oblander noted that program evaluation and attitude or opinion studies are the most frequent and that respondents were "generally somewhat dissatisfied" with the accessibility of data for decision-making purposes.

Administrators who say there isn't time or money to do research are being short-sighted at best. It is a question of priorities and it is a question of realizing that devoting staff time and budgeting money for research and evaluation purposes can lead to more efficiencies, cost savings, and more impact. I have been quoted in several places earlier in this monograph as propounding that "research is an obligation, not a frill" (Brown, 1986, p. 195). I cannot say it any other way. I believe wholeheartedly that the chief campus student affairs administrators are the "who" when we ask, "Who needs to be doing something?" The earlier chapters provide an excellent context for administrators and others in the profession to be inspired and activated to launch a research agenda on their campuses. I hope it does.

What Needs to be Done?

I believe that campus administrators are ultimately responsible for seeing that the following actions are taken. However, no matter what role you have in the profession, you can help. Here is my list:

1. Declare a moratorium on surveys and grade prediction studies. No surveys or grade prediction studies should be

conducted on the campus level unless they are directly tied to an intervention program. That is, a survey of student drinking behaviors might be given before and after a residence education program on alcohol abuse. Or, a grade prediction study might be conducted prior to establishing a program to identify and work directly with high-risk students. Journal editors should refuse to accept manuscripts for publication that are primarily survey data unless the researchers tie the data directly to programmatic evaluation efforts or unless the researchers provide documentation that the results have led to program changes and improvements.

2. Form a campus screening committee for research projects. Each campus should have a screening committee that reviews and passes judgment on what questionnaires or surveys can be mailed to students or distributed in classes. Too much student time is wasted completing poorly designed instruments for inadequately conceptualized studies. This committee should consist of faculty, student affairs, and student representatives. The restrictions should apply to faculty conducting research as well as to student affairs staff members. Student affairs offices control sponsored bulletin boards; do the same for surveys.

This committee should also serve a proactive role to help determine what program evaluation studies, needs assessments, or other studies should be conducted. Students serve on program planning and speaker selection groups; let's do the same with research and evaluation studies.

3. Develop a research mindset for making decisions. Preface every new policy statement or program change with a question, "What does the research literature have to say on this topic?" Past personal experiences and intuition are fine and can be part of the decision-making and planning process, but so must available research findings. This does not mean decision makers or researchers must slavishly follow research evidence, but at least they should be aware of what was done before, where, and what the findings were.

4. Institute a policy that every administrator must be a participant with his or her staff in at least one meaningful research study each year. If the administrator does not have the time to participate in at least some small way in a research project each year, it provides a clear message to the rest of the staff that research must not be all that important. The administrator does not have to lead or direct a research project, but participation at any level can provide an excellent model for all staff.

Whether a student affairs unit has a central research office, I believe that research activities should be infused throughout student affairs rather than relegated solely to a central office. Practitioners will never fulfill the ideal of the scientist-practitioner model if they rely exclusively on a central office. And, a central office staff will usually find the impact of their efforts are directly related to the amount of involvement that other staff have in the planning, conducting, and interpreting the research studies.

5. Make participation in research projects an integral part of the reward system in student affairs. Job descriptions for student affairs positions need to include participation in research projects, and annual staff evaluations should look at this as an important dimension. How can research activities increase on campuses when participation in research projects is largely ignored as a criterion for when and pay raises? Psychologists have long known that one of the best ways to eliminate or extinguish a behavior is to ignore it. Why be surprised then that research activities have not increased in student affairs? This is clearly an example of the absolute necessity that chief student affairs officers provide tangible support for research within their administrative province.

6. Focus systematic research efforts on outcome assessment and program improvement. Too much of student affairs assessment focuses on what I call "happiness indices." Too often assessment focuses on determining whether students were satisfied and whether they think they learned

something. Outcome assessment needs to be targeted to program goals. That means that goals for student affairs need to be articulated in language more specific than the rhetoric of the customary mission statements. And, while everyone hopes students are satisfied and believe they learned something, researchers need to work harder at getting objective as well as subjective data about what they learned or how they changed. Student affairs staffs need to ask appropriate questions. What do we expect students to get out of the experience of living in the residence halls? What are the expectancies for the emerging leader training program? What skills are student government leaders or health aides supposed to learn as a result of their role? What is the environment of a good residence hall supposed to be like? How many students need and have financial aid or work-study positions?

This is not to say that unintended positive effects of programs and services are to be ignored. Sometimes goals change and new goals emerge. Administrators and staff must be alert to changing needs and be flexible enough to make the necessary changes in expected outcomes and be creative enough to find new ways to assess them. But certainly, program planners have expectations about outcomes, and there are ways to measure or at least obtain indicators of many anticipated outcomes (Hanson, 1982; Tinsley & Irelan, 1989). Also, see Hanson's comments in Chapter Five. Having access to outcome data makes it easier to determine the impact of planned and unplanned program changes and provides a solid foundation for being accountable for what student affairs members do (Madson, Benedict & Weitzer, 1989; Weitzer & Malaney, Chapter Three).

Data collection aimed at program improvement should also be an integral part of every program and every student affairs unit. For this purpose, the process may be less formal and less formidable than for accountability purposes. No matter what the student affairs unit is or what the program is, the administration and staff must constantly ask themselves: How can we do it better? How can we reach more students? How can we be more cost effective?

Data to answer these questions might consist primarily of staff opinions and observations or the data might include student opinion. This is a process that may begin as early as the first hour of a new registration process, the first half-day of a three-day workshop, or the first month of a new floor government organization. What data are collected, how, and when are important issues, but more central to improvement is having an expectation and process whereby the program or unit is continually looking for ways to improve. Program evaluation should not be an event that occurs only for special programs or only when the spotlight swings in that unit's direction; rather, program evaluation should be part of a unit's way of life, a constant mindset that entails searching for ways to improve practice.

Verdict and Reform

I'm obviously not sanguine about the past or present status of research in student affairs. But neither am I pessimistic. I think the enthusiasm is present and the need has been acknowledged. As this monograph notes, the necessary tools are increasingly available and with some imagination a research program could be nearly cost free. Student affairs professionals must now follow through on the commitment that is necessary.

If you are in a position to change the status of research in student affairs, and I believe every reader who has gotten this far in this monograph is in such a position, you are now more morally culpable than you were before you started this monograph. Now you know what has gone wrong. The excuses have been used up. And now you must take a course of action or be guilty of negligence. Assuming that everyone has a measure of guilt, including myself, we might as well skip the verdict, like I have in this chapter, and begin the reform. I will start myself before somebody decides to put the judge on trial.

References

Beeler, K.J., and Oblander, F.W. (1989). A study of student affairs research and evaluation activities in American colleges and universities. Unpublished report. Washington, DC: National Association of Student Personnel Administrators, Inc.

Berdie, R.F. (1966). Student personnel work: Definition and redefinition. ACPA presidential address. *Journal of College Student Personnel,* 7, 146-56.

Brown, R.D. (1972). Student personnel research: Ivory tower or the new specialty? *Journal of the National Association of Women Deans, Administrators, and Counselors,* 35(4) 171-77.

Brown, R.D. (1978). Implications of new evaluation strategies for accountability in student affairs. *Journal of College Student Personnel,* 19(2), 123-26.

Brown, R.D. (1980). Evaluating campus learning centers. In O.T. Lenning and R.L. Nayan (eds.), *New roles for learning assistance* (pp. 75-92). New Directions in College Learning Assistant, No. 2. San Francisco: Jossey-Bass Publisher, Inc.

Brown, R.D. (1983). Editorial: A common vision. *Journal of College Student Personnel,* 24, 3-5.

Brown, R.D. (1986). Research: A frill or an obligation? *Journal of College Student Personnel,* 27(3), 195.

Brown, R.D. (1987). Evaluating counseling centers. In J.F. Wergin and L.A. Braskamp (eds), *Evaluating administrative services and programs* (pp. 59-69). New Directions for Institutional Research, No. 56. San Francisco: Jossey-Bass Publisher, Inc.

Brown, R.D., and Sanstead, M.J. (1982). Using evaluation to make decisions about academic advising programs. In R. Winston, S. Ender, and T. Miller (eds.), *Development advising* (pp. 55-66). New Directions for Student Services, No. 17. San Francisco: Jossey-Bass Publisher, Inc.

CAS (1986). *CAS standards and guidelines for student services/development programs.* Iowa City, IA: ACT.

Hanson, G. (ed.). (1982). *Measuring student development.* New Directions for Student Services, No. 20. San Francisco: Jossey-Bass Publisher, Inc.

Kuh, G.D. (1979). *Evaluation in student affairs.* Cincinnati: American College Personnel Association.

Kuh, G.; Lardy, B.A.; and Greenlee, F. (1979). Research orientation of graduate students in college student personnel. *Journal of College Student Personnel,* 20, 99-104.

Johnson, D.H., and Steele, B.H. (1984). A national survey of research activity and attitudes in student affairs divisions. *Journal of College Student Personnel,* 25(3), 200-05.

Madson, D.L.; Benedict, L.G; and Weitzer, W.H. (1989). Using information systems for decision making and planning. In U. Delworth and G.R. Hanson (eds.), *Student services: A handbook for the profession* (2nd ed.). San Francisco: Jossey-Bass Publisher, Inc.

Meara, N.M. (1990). 1989 division 17, presidential address. *The Counseling Psychologist,* 18(1), 144-67.

Moxley, L.S. (1988). The role and impact of a student affairs research and evaluation office. *NASPA Journal,* 25(3), 174-79.

NASPA (1987). *A perspective on student affairs.* Washington, DC: National Association of Student Personnel Administrators, Inc.

Tinsley, D.J., and Irelan, T.M. (1989). Instruments used in college student affairs research: an analysis of the measurement base of a young profession. *Journal of College Student Development,* 30(5), 440-47.

NASPA Publications
ORDER FORM

	Quantity	Cost		Quantity	Cost
The Role of Student Affairs in Institution-Wide Enrollment Management Strategies $7.95 members, $9.95 nonmembers	_____	_____	Private Dreams, Shared Visions: Student Affairs Work in Small Colleges. $5.95 members, $7.50 nonmembers	_____	_____
The Invisible Leaders: Student Affairs Mid-manager $7.95 members, $9.95 nonmembers	_____	_____	Translating Theory into Practice: Implications of Japanese Management Theory for Student Personnel Administrators. $5.95 members, $7.50 nonmembers	_____	_____
The New Professional: A Resource Guide for New Student Affairs Professionals and Their Supervisors. $7.95 members, $9.95 nonmembers	_____	_____	Risk Management and the Student Affairs Professional. $5.95 members, $7.50 nonmembers	_____	_____
From Survival to Success: Promoting Minority Student Retention. $7.95 members, $9.95 nonmembers	_____	_____	Career Perspectives in Student Affairs. $5.95 members, $7.50 nonmembers	_____	_____
Student Affairs and Campus Dissent. $5.95 members, $7.50 nonmembers	_____	_____	Points of View. $5 members, $7 nonmembers	_____	_____
Alcohol Policies and Procedures on College and University Campuses $5.95 members, $7.50 nonmembers	_____	_____	NASPA Journal, $35 annual subscription, $9.50 single copy. If single issue, indicate volume and issue: _____	_____	_____
Opportunities for Student Development in Two-Year Colleges. $5.95 members, $7.50 nonmembers	_____	_____	TOTAL	_____	_____

Please return completed form with check, money order, or credit card authorization. Return to: NASPA, 1875 Connecticut Avenue, NW, Suite 418, Washington, D.C. 20009-5728; (202) 265-7500.

Payment enclosed ☐ Bill my credit card ☐

VISA ☐ MasterCard ☐ Expiration Date _____

Account Number _____ Signature _____

Please Print

Name _____ NASPA Membership ID No. _____

Address _____

City _____ State _____ Zip _____